HEALTH & FITNESS TIPS TO IMPROVE YOUR GOLF

Every Golfer's Guide on How
to Enjoy Better Golf,
Prevent Injuries,
and Improve
Fitness.

George C. Giam, M.D.

Foreword by

Gary Player

Published by Fit-Golf & More (U.S.A.),
the golf division of Fit-Sport & More (U.S.A.), Inc.
Los Angeles, California, U.S.A.

"*More people should train to play and not play to train. This book instructs golfers of all levels to prepare physically and mentally to play the game.*"
–Professor James S. Skinner, Ph.D., Director, Exercise and Sports Research Institute, Arizona State University, and Past-President, American College of Sports Medicine.

"Adopting the elegantly simplified directions in Dr. Giam's book, golfers should improve and be more consistent in their game as well as live healthier lives."
– Professor Brent S. Rushall, Ph.D., Department of Exercise and Nutritional Sciences, San Diego State University, California, and consultant to World and Olympic Games athletes in many sports, including golf.

Par 3, 8th Hole, Mission Hills North Golf Course, Rancho Mirage, California

More (U.S.A.),
& More (U.S.A.), Inc.
Los Angeles
03, U.S.A.
Tel: 1-800-9-FIT-GOLF or 1-800-934-8465
Tel: (213) 550-8886 • Fax: (213) 550-8887

PRINTED AND BOUND IN THE UNITED STATES OF AMERICA
10 9 8 7 6 5 4 3 2 1
First printed in April 1995

Library of Congress Catalog Card Number 95-90284
Dr. George C. Giam
Health & Fitness Tips To Improve Your Golf
1. Fitness   2. Golf
Includes references and index

ISBN 1-887384-00-6 (for soft cover version)

FOREWORD

by

Gary Player

(Winner of more than 150 golf tournaments
including three U.S. Masters, three British Opens,
two P.G.A. Championships, the U.S. Open, and
both the Regular and Senior Grand Slams of golf.)

I am honored that I have been asked to write a dedication for Dr. George Giam's outstanding book. Not only is the material first class, but Dr. Giam is one of the finest gentlemen I have met.

This book professionally and enjoyably covers a wide range of topics. It's almost everything a person needs to know about health.

I found fascinating the information on the heart and diabetes, advice for the fit golfer, and those still striving to get in shape.

This book is filled with vast sums of knowledge that I know you'll find useful. I strongly recommend this book, and I trust you'll enjoy it as much as I do.

CONTENTS

DEDICATION

This book is dedicated to all golfers who share
my passion (or is it "craziness" or "addiction") for
this challenging yet frustrating game. It is
particularly dedicated to those golfers who have
not yet realized how a better level of health and
fitness can help them to significantly improve their golf,
and enjoy their chosen passion even more.

ACKNOWLEDGMENTS

I am grateful for the very strong support and kind words about this book and me that Mr. Gary Player has expressed in his Foreword to this book. His inspiration as a true gentleman, golfer par excellence, and an outstanding example of health and fitness, has made him one of golf's greatest legends and international ambassadors of golf and fitness. To date, Mr. Player has won over 150 golf tournaments around the globe and is one of only four golfers to have won all the four major championships –three U.S. Masters, three British Opens, two P.G.A. Championships, and the U.S. Open. He is also the only man this century to have won the British Open in three decades (1959, 1968, and 1974), and both the Regular and Senior Grand Slams of golf.

Mr. Player has written many books on golf including the best-selling *"Golf Begins at 50"* and more recently *"Fit for Golf."* At his current age of 60 years, I know he is fitter than many professional golfers and other athletes half his age! His sincerity in wanting to help other golfers improve their game as well as their health and fitness, is rare among superstars past and present. That is why Mr. Player was the first and only person I requested to write the Foreword to this book because besides enjoying the game of golf, we share a common passion for wanting to help golfers improve their health and fitness.

I am grateful to my wife Elizabeth (a specialist physician and regular jogger, but only an occasional golfer) for the time and effort she spent helping me with all aspects of my book, especially reviewing the content and manuscript. Her expertise as a physician was very useful when she assisted me in researching recent medical articles and books for relevant health and fitness information for inclusion in this book.

I am also grateful to Brent S. Rushall, Ph.D., James S. Skinner, Ph.D., Kenneth H. Cooper, M.D., M.P.H., and a senior golf journalist with a leading golf publication for the very valuable time and effort they spent reviewing this book in great detail, and offering their expert opinions, constructive criticisms, and suggestions in every chapter. I engaged the very experienced golf journalist–who requested anonymity for himself and his magazine for personal and professional reasons–to help me to edit and rewrite every chapter to ensure that the medical, scientific, and other technical information in this book are presented in ways that appeal to golfers and is easily understood by lay readers. He also offered useful suggestions to the format and style for this book–many of which were accepted.

Dr. Brent Rushall is a Professor in the Department of Exercise and Nutritional Sciences at San Diego State University, California, U.S.A. He is also one of the most respected sports psychologists in the world and has published 26 books and over 230 articles, book chapters, and psychology tests. They include his recent books *"Training for Sports and Fitness"* and *"Mental Skills Training For Sports."* His academic recognitions have included the designation of being the founding scholar in **Behavioral Sports Psychology** and a world authority in **Coaching Science**. Professor Rushall has vast knowledge and experience from consulting with and assisting competitive athletes at all levels (including World and Olympic Games athletes) and in many sports (including golf). He is therefore very familiar with the psychological and physical problems recreational, amateur, and professional golfers have –and how to overcome them. The comments and suggestions that Dr. Rushall made in every chapter were extremely valuable and I gratefully accepted them, particularly those for Hole No. 9: Using Your Mind To Lower Your Golf Scores.

Dr. James Skinner is currently a Professor in the Department of Exercise Science and Physical Education, Arizona State University, Tempe, Arizona, U.S.A., and the Director of its Exercise and Sport Research Institute. He is also a Past-President of the American College of Sports Medicine. Professor Skinner is a world-renowned authority in the fields of health and fitness who has been invited to lecture in 37 countries. He is also an active researcher who has published more than 100 scientific papers and presented many more. Dr. Skinner made many very valuable comments and suggestions that I gratefully accepted, particularly those in Hole No. 4, 5, 7, and 8.

Dr. Kenneth Cooper is a physician who is acknowledged as the international leader in the health and fitness movement. A recipient of many awards and honors, he is the author of *"Aerobics"*–the landmark book that coined that term and started America running. Dr. Cooper's exclusive aerobics system and the 1.5 mile "Cooper Test" run are used world-wide. He is President and Founder of the Cooper Aerobics Center in Dallas, Texas, U.S.A., which includes the Cooper Clinic and the renowned Institute for Aerobics Research. More than 20 million of his twelve books have been sold in over forty languages, including his 1994 book– *"The Antioxidant Revolution."* I am grateful to Dr. Cooper for reviewing and permitting me to extract from this book some of the latest information on free radicals, antioxidants, diet, and exercise, that are of interest and relevance to golfers.

My thanks also go to the following for their significant contributions and assistance in the production of this book:

■ My 17-year old son Gerald, a competitive tennis player, occasional golfer, and an outstanding university student for helping me with my research and computer program for my manuscript.

- My 15-year old daughter Pamela, for her tolerance in putting up with my frequent unavailability to be with her on the numerous occasions when I was too involved with the research and writing of this book.
- Mr. Detlef M. Reck, General Manager of the Industry Hills Sheraton Resort and Conference Center in the City of Industry, California, U.S.A.; Ms. Jan Nolan, Director of Recreational Services and Sales; and Mr. Richard Stegall, PGA, Director of Golf, for their kind permission, cooperation, and the free use of their Resort's impressive facilities—including the challenging Dwight D. Eisenhower and Babe D. Zacharias golf courses—for all the outdoor instructional photography.
- Mr. John Herndon, PGA, the former General Manager and Head Professional of the Mission Hills North Golf Course, Rancho Mirage, California, U.S.A., and his successor, Mr. John Carson, PGA, for their kind permission to use the spectacular photograph of the eighth hole of this superb and immaculate desert course in the Palm Springs area.
- The Gary Player Group for the free use of their golf clubs and attire for the instructional photography. Special thanks to Mr. Thomas M. Kirkpatrick, President of Kirklander (of Dublin, Ohio and Greensboro, North Caroline, U.S.A.—designer, manufacturer, and distributor of quality cotton knit apparel including the Gary Player golf shirts), his Vice-President, Mr. David Alexander, and Operations/Customer Service Coordinator Ms. Michelle M. Murtagh, for their kind assistance.
- James K.S. Liu, Ph.D. and Ms. Hasmig Yazedjian of Trilogic, Inc., Pasadena, California, U.S.A.; and Mr. Ty Kirkpatrick of Front Door Publications, Irvine, California, U.S.A., for their assistance in the computerized design and layout of this book.
- Mr. Gary Galvan (a professional photographer from Pasadena, California, U.S.A.), Mr. Bryan Kent and Ms. Judy Peterson (the professional models) and Ms. Cyndra Dunn (a professional hair and make-up artist), all from the Los Angeles area in California, U.S.A., for their contributions to the photography in this book.
- All my friends and patients who are golfers, and others who gave me their valuable feedback, opinions, and suggestions as to what I should include and exclude in this book.

ABOUT THE AUTHOR

Dr. George C. Giam is a physician who has been in clinical practice specializing in preventive medicine, sports medicine, and fitness since 1974. Although currently working in Los Angeles, California, U.S.A., he received his formal training in these specialties in renowned sports medicine institutes in Germany when he was on a postgraduate scholarship awarded by the German Government. Dr. Giam had additional training in leading sports medicine centers in the U.S.A., Canada, Australia, Japan, Eastern and Western Europe.

In 1984, Dr. Giam completed a major in sports psychology when he was awarded the prestigious *Canadian Commonwealth Visiting Fellowship* by the Canadian Commonwealth Foundation and the Association of Universities and Colleges of Canada. He was honored with the *International Olympic Committee Sports Medicine Award* in 1989 when it was conferred on him for his outstanding national and international contributions to sports medicine.

Among his many professional appointments and involvements, Dr. Giam was a visiting consultant in orthopedic surgery at a university teaching hospital and a lecturer in exercise physiology to medical students and physicians undergoing postgraduate medical programs. He currently teaches sports medicine–especially in relation to golf–to university students and athletes in California, and is a member of the American College of Sports Medicine.

Dr. Giam is the main author of the book for all athletes entitled *"Sports Medicine, Exercise and Fitness: A Guide For Everyone,"* and has presented or published 69 medical and scientific papers. He has been actively involved in 75 research studies–including one on how to prevent and treat the different injuries and medical problems sustained by professional, amateur, and recreational golfers. This four-year study was completed recently, and much of the information in this book is derived from it.

Dr. Giam is an all-round athlete and was a high-level competitive tennis player in his younger days. In 1975, he started playing golf and became a very keen and competitive golfer, winning some tournaments at club level. Currently, at 48 years of age, Dr. Giam's golf and USGA handicap is not what it used to be, especially after he suffered a serious "slipped" disc–with sciatica–in his lower back in 1990. After successfully treating himself–without surgery and mainly with exercises–he continues to enjoy two or three rounds of golf nearly every week. Dr. Giam now plays to a handicap of about 12 as he usually scores in the low 80's during a good 18-hole round of golf–and occasionally even below 80 on exceptionally good days!

INTRODUCTION

I congratulate you for making the very wise decision to do something to improve your health and fitness–and golf. I started playing golf 20 years ago–soon after I began full-time clinical practice as a physician specializing in preventive medicine, sports medicine, and fitness. I was seeing an increasing number of professional, amateur, and recreational golfers with injuries and other medical problems. At that time, I could not understand why the golfers–much more so than the other athletes I treat–insisted that they continue to play, despite the fact that their injuries and their doctors' advice suggested otherwise. I then decided to play golf so that I could better understand the golfer's psyche and the game's biomechanics–which would also assist me treat my golfer patients more appropriately and thereby help them to recover faster.

When I first started playing golf, I thought the game couldn't be difficult. Many unathletic and out-of-shape men and women play it. They appeared to enjoy the game and didn't seem to have many problems. I was a high-level competitive tennis player and could accurately return a fast-moving tennis ball hit by my opponent–often while running at full speed. In golf, I didn't have to run nor worry that my opponent would hit the ball back and I would have to hit it again. That is why when I first started playing golf, I thought it would be a very easy game for me to excel in because I believed that I should have no difficulty hitting a stationary golf ball exactly where I want it to go.

How wrong I was! Compared with the many other sports I have played competitively or recreationally, I often find golf more difficult to play and score well. It can also be more frustrating and ego-deflating. During my 20 years of golf, I calculated I have hit at least 100,000 balls at the practice range and on the more than 200 different golf courses I've played on. The majority of these courses have fairly wide fairways and large greens so I can shoot in the low 80's or better during a good 18-hole round. But, I am still trying to figure out why I can't get the ball to go where I want it to most of the time! And, when I do, why can't I do it consistently? On the course I play on most frequently, I have made par several times on every one of the 18 holes–but never during the same round! The golf world is full of great golfers and good teachers who propose this method and that cure to improve your game. Some I agree with, some I do not, others I'm not sure.

Soon after I started playing golf seriously, I realized that this game is nowhere near as easy as it looks. I also observed that golfers make it even more difficult. Most golfers are prepared to spend countless hours at the practice range to try to improve their swing or lengthen their drives, or at the practice green to groove in their chips and putts. ***But, the majority*** *of high handicappers and recreational golfers do not realize the vital contribution their physical and mental health and fitness make to their game and score. Often these are the areas they neglect most and that is unfortunate because they are areas that these golfers can easily improve on in a relatively short period of time when compared with the months it usually takes to adopt and adapt to a new swing.* (Note: Throughout this book, for your convenience, the more important information and tips will be highlighted in bold and italics, or in colored shadow or captioned boxes. If you decide not to read every page initially, then you should at least try to read and follow these highlighted text, the 64 color photographs and their accompanying instructions.)

During a golf trip in 1990, I suffered a severe herniated or prolapsed ("slipped") lumbar intervertebral disc when I incorrectly lifted a heavy golf bag and suitcase. My age of 43 years then and previous lower back problems from rigorous participation in sports and physical activities–including military service–definitely contributed to the development of this "slipped disc." Although an MRI confirmed that a sizable disc prolapse was responsible for my excruciating lower back pain and sciatica, I decided against surgery as the first treatment option–a principle I have also practiced for my patients in my 23 years as a physician. *Using my expertise and experience in sports medicine and orthopedics, I prescibed for myself judicious rest, medication, physical therapy, and very intensive stretching and strengthening exercises, especially for the back. I also altered my golf swing to put less stress on my back–sacrificing about 20 yards off the tee. But my accuracy improved, my back didn't hurt much–and I developed a better short game.* Three months later, I was back to playing full competitive golf at club tournaments. Since then, I have been regularly playing two rounds of golf a week–scoring fairly consistently now to a handicap of about 12.

In 1988, I wrote a book for health professionals and athletes entitled ***"Sports Medicine, Exercise And Fitness: A Guide For Everyone".*** Friends and patients who were golfers suggested that I follow up with a book specially designed to help golfers. In response to this suggestion and because of my continuing desire to share my professional and personal experiences with golf-related injuries and other medical problems, the idea for this book was born. *Most golfers are not sufficiently fit, nor do they wish to engage in a strenuous program of exercise. Golfers often have injuries and other medical problems, and would enjoy their game more if only they would follow a few simple tips to improve their and fitness–and this book is designed for that purpose.*

Although it is ideal that golfers read this book from the first page to the last, some of you may not be interested in all the different topics outlined in the nine chapters–called holes in this book to reflect the flavor of golf. I have therefore written this book so that you can read each chapter independently. For this reason, I have repeated the more important information and tips in the different chapters (e.g., preventing and treating lower back problems in Hole No. 5 and 8).

I engaged a very experienced senior golf journalist with a leading golf magazine to go through in detail the original manuscript of my book and to rewrite all sentences or sections that were presented too technically. *This is to ensure that the medical and scientific tips and information in this book are presented in ways that appeal to golfers and are easily understood by lay readers.* I also made it a point to include some humor in certain areas–because too many golfers are overly serious about anything involving their game. But, you should not misinterpret this to mean that the health and fitness tips, suggestions, and recommendations I share with you should not be taken seriously.

Based on my professional and personal experiences, and the feedback from fellow golfers, I believe I have provided all the useful information that most golfers like you would probably need. However, it is impossible to provide answers or solutions to all the health and fitness needs of every golfer in a book of this size and nature. If you need more details or information, you should refer to the selected publications listed at the end of this book under References and Recommended Publications for Further Reading. The most recommended ones are Mr. Gary Player's *"Fit For Golf: 100 Exercises To Improve Your Game"*, Dr. Brent Rushall's *"Mental Skills Training For Sports"*, and Dr. Kenneth Cooper's *"The Antioxidant Revolution."* I welcome any comments or suggestions from you, your fellow golfers, or my fellow health professionals that would make future editions of this book even more helpful to you and other golfers of every skill level.

Whatever your current state of health, fitness, and golf, I am confident that this book will provide you with sufficient tips, advice, and information that would be useful to you. Improving your health and fitness will definitely enhance your effectiveness in any round of golf and extend the number of years that you can play without significant pain or ill-health. To a large extent, you can prevent such injuries and disability from happening to you by following tips in this book.

I wish you all success in your endeavor to achieve a healthier and fitter body and mind so that you can play better golf and enjoy this very challenging passion of ours even though it can sometimes turn out to be an exercise in frustration!

George C. Giam, M.D.   April 1995
4917 Glacier Drive, Los Angeles
California 90041-2403, U.S.A.

HOLE NO. 1

WHY GOLFERS NEED THIS BOOK– SOME BACKGROUND INFORMATION

> ■ How better health and fitness can improve
> your golf and lower your score
> ■ Golf-related injuries and deaths–how they occur

HOW BETTER HEALTH AND FITNESS CAN IMPROVE YOUR GOLF AND LOWER YOUR SCORE

Would you like to hit your tee shots more than 20 yards farther, improve your accuracy, and cut at least two strokes off your score? Of course, you would. However, it's simply not that easy–regardless of news of the latest high-tech driver, the golf ball that promises extra distance, or the new biomechanically-correct golf swing.

But one sure and easy way to longer, straighter shots, and lower scores–without even having to change your swing–is to improve the physical condition of your body and the mental attitude of your mind.

Golf is not a strenuous game. However, it can be physically demanding if you are unfit. Do you have lower back pain? Does your elbow or wrist ache? Do your shoulders or knees give you problems? If your answer to any of these questions is "Yes," then following even some of the advice and tips in this book will definitely help you.

While golfers are notorious for their unwillingness to exercise, they only have to look to the more successful professionals for the benefits of better physical conditioning. The Senior PGA Tour players are using physical fitness to achieve better golf. They know that increased strength and flexibility mean longer, straighter shots.

A University of Oregon study found that a 20-yard increase in tee-shot distance reduced the golf score by at least two strokes per round. "Sports Coach" reported that the accuracy threshold of golf shots is 85% to 90% of your maximum swing.

Therefore, with the same swing, if you have increased strength and flexibility, you can gain extra distance without loss of accuracy. Furthermore, better health and fitness means you can enjoy your game for a longer time and with fewer interruptions due to pain, injury, or ill-health. All these benefits should be very attractive to golfers like you.

GOLF-RELATED INJURIES AND HOW THEY OCCUR

If you are in pain, it's your body's signal that something is wrong–and you should slow down, or even stop what you are doing. Unfortunately, many golfers stubbornly play their way through the pain. That kind of thinking is wrong–and may sometimes be dangerous.

Pain means injury or other significant medical problems. It also means that the injured part of your body–which is weaker than normal–is not fit enough to do what it normally can. Therefore, an injury needs treatment and judicious rest–but not necessarily complete rest. Please refer to the end of Hole No. 6 for further information on "Should you stop playing golf when injured?"

Golf-related injuries can occur in the following forms:

- Strains–partial tears of muscle or tendon (e.g., tendinitis) with occasional ruptures or complete tears.
- Sprains–partial tears of the ligaments or capsules of joint (e.g., ankle sprains) with occasional ruptures or complete tears.
- Lower back problems–usually due to partial tears of ligaments and muscles (often with spasm). However, "slipped" discs are not uncommon, especially among golfers who are unfit, overweight, or past 40 years of age.
- Fractures and dislocations–occur very occasionally and usually not directly from swinging the golf club but from falls and other accidents.

A golf injury usually occurs after a sudden, incorrect movement in your golf swing. Often it happens on the practice tee when golfers, as is their bad habit, hit a large number of balls in rapid succession without sufficient or proper warm-up.

They get out of the car, rush for the range, and immediately start hitting buckets of balls with full swings. They don't give a thought to warming up their muscles and ligaments properly before subjecting them to such rigors. Players like these are begging for injuries.

Even golfers who don't warm up properly before an 18-hole round aren't as vulnerable to such injuries. This is because they do not hit as many full shots over a 4- to 5-hour round (usually fewer than 36–for the drive and fairway shots)–and at a rate of one every several minutes).

Compare this with the 50 to 100 balls (or more) that many golfers pound at the range in 30 to 60 minutes–a rate of one every 15 to 30 seconds!

Such a routine at the practice range–if repeated several times each month and for years–will result in recurrent and chronic injuries. Such injuries will be detrimental to the golfer's game. They may also be severe enough to require some golfers to discontinue playing for weeks–or even months.

Most golf injuries occur during the downswing (the "hitting phase"), either just before or during impact with the ball or ground. Injuries next most commonly happen after impact (during the "follow through" phase) and least commonly occur during the start of the swing (the "take away" phase).

In their study of 393 injuries among golf professionals, McCarroll and Gioe showed that:

- About 70% occur due to repetitive golf swing–e.g., practicing, teaching, or demonstrating at the practice range.
- About 20% occur because of contact with firm objects other than the golf ball–e.g., stones, tree roots, hard rubber mats at the practice range, firm sand in traps, taking divots on hard ground.
- The remaining 10% were injuries–e.g., twisting an ankle–due to other activities like slipping on slopes, stepping into small pot-holes, or falling when walking on very uneven ground.

A recent detailed study of 136 injuries among professional, amateur, and recreational golfers seen at my sports medicine clinic revealed that about:

- 52% involved the upper limbs–mostly "golfer's elbow," "tennis elbow," and wrist injuries.
- 24% were lower back problems–including some "slipped" discs.
- The remaining 24% affected the lower limbs (mainly the knee and ankle), neck, and the rest of the body.
- 80% of all the golf injuries in this study were relatively minor injuries to muscles and tendons.
- 19% were relatively minor injuries to the ligaments and joints.
- The remaining 1% consisted mainly of contusions and bruises, with the occasional "slipped" disc, dislocation, or fracture.

For more information, please refer to further details of this study that was published as a scientific paper entitled ***"Prevention and Treatment of Common Golf Injuries"*** in Sports Medicine News. This is a publication for physicians and other health professionals, and is one of the recommended references for further reading listed at the end of this book.

Most injuries and other medical problems in golf can easily be prevented, or their risk of developing greatly reduced. But that can only be accomplished if you pay more attention to maintaining or improving your health and fitness. Simple warm-up, stretching, and strengthening exercises (as presented in the other chapters in this book) can add yards to your shots and years to your golf career. Like anything else worthwhile, the key is preparation and practice!

GOLF-RELATED DEATHS

Golf is a safe game–even for the unfit. That is why death on the golf course is rare. Unfortunately, when it does occur, it is very unlikely that you will forget what you may have heard–or witnessed. However, for every golfer who dies while playing golf, there are hundreds of thousands of golfers and non-golfers who die in their sleep or while doing other non-golfing activities.

The most common deaths that occur while playing golf are due to heart attacks. These usually happen to older or unfit golfers with known or unknown heart disease. Less frequent golf-related deaths that have been reported are those due to lightning strikes, heat stroke, snake bites, and electrocution from fallen power lines.

All these known causes of deaths while playing golf are often preventable. All you need to do is to follow the important information and tips provided in this book about how to improve your health, fitness, and prevent problems like dehydration. You should also learn to recognize and heed your body's warning signs and symptoms–e.g., breathlessness and chest pains before a heart attack.

Taking precautionary measures–e.g., carrying in your golf bag any emergency medication you are taking–are some other advice that will be discussed in greater detail in Hole No. 3: Preparing Yourself For A Round Of Golf.

Comply with signals and warnings to take cover and discontinue playing golf when there is lightning. Heed warning signs about the presence of poisonous snakes in areas where your golf ball may have strayed.

This is some common sense advice that all golfers should take more seriously.

HOLE NO. 2

YOUR GOLF ALSO DEPENDS ON WHAT YOU EAT OR DRINK

- What to eat before, during, and after your game
- Carbohydrates, proteins, fats, minerals, vitamins, free radicals, and antioxidants
- Fluids and electrolytes
- Smoking and tobacco

WHAT TO EAT BEFORE, DURING, AND AFTER YOUR GAME

How many times have you set out for a round of golf and done one or more of the following:

- Grabbed a quick cup of coffee and headed for the door.
- Wolfed down a hot dog or sandwich at the golf course ten minutes before tee time.
- Decided not to eat at all until after the round.

Sound familiar? Then it shouldn't be surprising that on those occasions you stuck to these poor dietary habits, your round of golf often ended badly. You felt tired, your energy was gone, your concentration was poor, and those last few shots weren't struck with much power. *Believe it or not, what and when you eat and drink can be just as vital to your golf score as your equipment or swing.*

It's recommended that you eat a normal and familiar breakfast (or lunch), preferably at least two or three hours before the start of your round of golf. *Your pre-game meal should not be high in fats or proteins as such a meal usually takes a longer time to digest–than the usual two to three hours.* Playing golf with excess undigested food in your stomach is unlikely to help you play well. It's also not a good idea to try new foods or drinks during this meal as they may irritate your digestive system. You certainly don't want to visit the restroom after every few holes.

If you need just a snack before or during a round of golf, choose one that is high in carbohydrates, and low in fats and proteins. Examples are chocolate bars, candy bars, fruits–or a handful of raisins as Gary Player reportedly eats. The reason is that such snacks are easily and rapidly digested, and provide quick relief from hunger and low blood sugar (hypoglycemia). After your round, you should eat higher amounts of proteins and fats to ensure that you have a nutritionally balanced diet for that day. But do keep a watch on your total intake of calories and nutrients.

CARBOHYDRATES, PROTEINS, FATS, MINERALS, VITAMINS, FREE RADICALS, AND ANTIOXIDANTS

The following overall dietary recommendations for general health, fitness, and disease risk reduction are consistent with recent World Health Organization's (WHO) guidelines:

- Daily intake of complex carbohydrates–e.g., from wheat, potato, and rice–should be about 50% to 70% of total energy intake.
- Processed sugar–e.g., those found in refined sugar and sweets–should constitute less than 10% of total daily energy intake.
- Restrict daily total fat intake to 15% to 30% of total energy intake, and daily cholesterol intake to less than about 300 mg.
- Daily protein should be 10% to 15% of total energy intake.
- Adequate daily intake of water, and if you consume alcohol, limit daily intake to low and safe levels–e.g., for driving.
- Restrict daily salt intake to less than about 6 gm–or about 2.4 gm of sodium–by reducing intake of salt and salt-cured foods.
- Ensure high daily intake of fruit, vegetables, and whole grain cereals, thereby having sufficient intake of vitamins like A and C, and fiber intake and roughage to ensure proper digestion.
- Eat a variety of foods.

If you regularly have a balanced diet from various nutritional sources (e.g., different types of vegetables, fruits, bread, and other wheat products, rice, meat, fish, eggs, milk, and other dairy products), you probably would be taking in at least the minimum amounts of vitamins and minerals as recommended by the U.S. Food and Drug Administration (FDA). However, this is provided you do not overcook your food–which can destroy many nutrients–or have any digestive system or absorption disorders.

Until recently, many physicians, dietitians, and nutritionists advocated that you need not take any vitamin or mineral supplements if you have an overall well-balanced diet. My view has been that if you are unsure whether you are getting the minimum as recommended by the FDA, it is acceptable to take one multivitamin tablet daily but there was no need to take megadoses. However, this thinking is being challenged by recent scientific research that have uncovered new evidence on the possible toxic effect on your body of certain unstable oxygen molecules called free radicals, and how their adverse effects can be counteracted by certain substances called antioxidants.

I am grateful to Kenneth H. Cooper, M.D., M.P.H., for reviewing and permitting me to extract from his 1994 book "*The Antioxidant Revolution*" some of the latest information on free radicals, antioxidants, diet, and exercise, that are of particular interest and relevance to golfers. For more information, please read his book and other recommended references listed at the end of this book. Dr. Cooper is a physician who has received many awards and honors. He is the President and Founder of the Cooper Aerobics Center in Dallas, Texas, U.S.A., which includes the Cooper Clinic and the renowned Institute for Aerobics Research. He is an international leader in health and fitness, and more than 20 million of his twelve books have been sold in over forty languages.

Antioxidants can be produced by your body (endogenous antioxidants) or you can get them from your diet or vitamin supplements (exogenous antioxidants). *The most important of these exogenous antioxidants are Vitamin C, Vitamin E, and beta carotene–the carotenoid precursor to Vitamin A.* In controlled proportions, free radicals play important roles in keeping you healthy. For example, they contribute to the maintenance of the optimal tone of your blood vessels, and assist in the defense of the body against infection and inflammation. There is, however, a delicate balance between the good and harmful effects of free radicals.

Excess free radicals have been associated with:

- Atherosclerosis–the hardening of arteries that contribute to coronary artery disease.
- Cell damage that may lead to various cancers–e.g., lung, bladder, rectal cancers and skin melanomas.
- Impaired immunity resulting in an increased incidence of viral colds and other infections.
- Premature aging and the formation of cataracts.

The release of excess free radicals in your body is triggered by causes which are so much a part of your current environment and lifestyle habits. For example, UV light produced by the sun, air pollution (e.g., from cigarette smoke), contaminants in food, and even excessive exercising!

Antioxidants are believed to help protect your body against the harmful effects of these excess free radicals. Recent studies have shown that to be of use, antioxidants have to be taken in far larger amounts than can be obtained from a normal balanced diet, and what is contained in the usual multivitamin supplements. Dr. Cooper now recommends daily doses of 1,000 mg of Vitamin C, 400 to 600 I.U. (International Units) of Vitamin E, and 25,000 to 50,000 I.U. of beta carotene for adult females who are not over 200 lbs or heavy exercisers. For adult males who are not over 200 lbs or heavy exercisers, he recommends daily doses of 1,500 to 2,000 mg of Vitamin C, 400 to 600 I.U. of Vitamin E, and 25,000 to 50,000 I.U. of beta carotene. Other authorities recommend lower daily doses–250 mg to 500 mg of Vitamin C (because some believe that the body excretes any in excess of 400 mg), 100 to 400 I. U. of Vitamin E, and 25,000 to 40,000 I. U. of beta carotene.

Some words of caution, though. *Current medical and scientific studies show no significant benefits if you take doses higher than those recommended.* Furthermore, for some adults, taking one or more of these antioxidants may also produce side effects that can be potentially harmful. For instance, Vitamin E, which has an anti-clotting effect in your blood is not recommended if you are on anti-coagulant therapy (e.g., coumarin, aspirin–which may be prescribed to those with some types of heart disease). Some studies also suggest that high doses of Vitamin E may increase plasma lipids (fat).

Relatively high doses of Vitamin C – e.g., more than 4,000 mg daily –may result in loose bowels or diarrhea in some people. If you have a history of kidney stones, you should also be careful about taking excess Vitamin C because it is soluble in water, excreted through the kidney, and may increase the risk of kidney stones. Tablets of Vitamin C (ascorbic acid) that can be swallowed rather than have to be chewed are preferred because chewing them may make the mouth acid enough to start dissolving your tooth enamel.

Toxic effects of beta carotene have not been reported in normal, healthy people except when taken by heavy smokers, or with relatively large amounts of alcohol–which may result in more severe liver damage. According to Dr. Cooper, there are no definitive studies now that tell us how much alcohol you can take safely with beta carotene. If you take beta carotene, he recommends no more than one ounce per day of pure alcohol–which is equivalent to about two average-sized, four ounce glasses of wine, two beers, or one mixed drink! Dr. Cooper also emphasizes that under no circumstances should you take beta carotene if you drink more than four to six ounces of pure alcohol per day.

It is best that you consult a physician who is familiar with recent medical and scientific information on antioxidants before embarking on a regime of large doses. To prevent possibly dangerous drug interactions, you should also inform your physician about vitamin and other supplements you are taking.

One of the biggest myths regarding sports nutrition is the belief that large amounts of proteins are necessary for good performance. Athletes in events requiring predominantly strength, have been known to eat large amounts of proteins, particularly beef, because they believe it will make them stronger. If only they would remember that even the strongest bulls survive almost exclusively on a diet of grass, which has a protein content much less than in the normal diet of all but the poorest people in the world today. (**Note**: I am not suggesting that you eat grass exclusively because the human digestive system is not as efficient in digesting and extracting nutrients from grass.)

Proteins are not used as fuels for energy to any appreciable extent–so long as energy supplies from carbohydrates and fats are adequate. Proteins, however, are necessary for the building, maintenance, and repair of body tissues, including muscles. The golfer involved in rigorous training and competition will definitely require more protein. It is even more important if he or she is trying to develop more muscles through a resistance or weight-training program, or is a growing adolescent. However, even in such golfers, a two-fold increase in dietary protein from the normal non-athlete's protein requirements can easily be met by an increased intake of a balanced diet. Therefore, there is no real need to resort to protein supplements (e.g., protein tablets) if you eat a well-balanced diet.

Should doubt exist regarding whether a diet is well balanced, and protein supplements are indicated, then dairy products like milk and cheese, and animal proteins and eggs, are recommended, rather than protein tablets. These natural foods usually are less expensive per unit of protein content, contain other essential nutrients like vitamins, minerals, carbohydrates, and fats, and have other benefits–e.g., provide bulk and satisfy your hunger sensation.

Protein intake in excess of daily requirements only results in more work for your liver and kidneys, as they have to break down and excrete the excess proteins. The reason is that proteins–unlike carbohydrates and fats–cannot be stored to any appreciable extent in your body, and the excess has to be excreted mainly through the urine and feces. Therefore, excess protein intake is of no value and may even be detrimental to your health and golf. The increased health risks include the possibility of liver and kidney disorders, and other conditions like gout (high uric acid). Excess protein intake is more expensive, is less efficient as fuel for energy than carbohydrates and fats, and can induce dehydration, loss of appetite, and diarrhea.

FLUIDS AND ELECTROLYTES

Drink as much fluid as you can before and during your round of golf. It is better to visit the restroom every few hours than to be dehydrated and try to play with cramped fingers or calf muscles. **Guidelines from the**

American College of Sports Medicine (ACSM) and fluid requirements in golf suggest that the recommended minimum for golfers is a quarter to a half cup of fluids 15 to 30 minutes before the game starts, and every 15 to 30 minutes during the game. You should drink more if you are losing excessive sweat during a particular game or day.

Plain water is the best drink because when you sweat, you lose mainly water–with just a very small amount of salt and other electrolytes. Furthermore, water is more rapidly absorbed than most other fluids–e.g., sweetened drinks like soft drinks, sodas, coffee, and tea. If you are losing a lot of sweat, then adding just a pinch of table salt–not a half teaspoonful but just grains of salt you can pick up between your thumb and index finger–in a glass of water is usually enough. Many of the commercial "isotonic" or "electrolyte replacer" drinks have about twice the minimum recommended electrolyte content set out in the ACSM guidelines.

Be aware that in hot-dry or windy conditions, you may be losing a lot more fluid than you realize. This is because the sweat you produce evaporates very quickly when the humidity is low or the wind is strong. You should therefore drink about as much fluids as you normally would during a hot-humid or windless day when you sweat continuously and are aware of it as the sweat remains on your skin or clothes because it takes a much longer time to evaporate.

Whenever possible, avoid drinks with alcohol or caffeine–e.g., tea, coffee, colas–before and during a round of golf because they may help in dehydrating rather than hydrating you. The reason is that alcohol and caffeine have diuretic effects, and therefore make your body produce more urine, lose more water, and visit the restroom more often. Alcohol is also a central nervous system depressant–not a stimulant as many golfers think –and golf requires a clear and sharp mind and body, not a dull and sleepy one.

SMOKING AND TOBACCO

Tobacco, whether smoked or chewed, should be avoided, especially during golf. The nicotine and other chemicals in tobacco overstimulate the cardiovascular, nervous, and muscular systems. This may result in a tense and anxious golfer with a pounding heart and shaky hands–which are not conducive to good golf!

HOLE NO. 3

PREPARING YOURSELF
FOR A ROUND OF GOLF

- Get ready the day before
- What to wear
- The skin game–skin care and skin care tips

GET READY THE DAY BEFORE

"Golf is a tough game made even more difficult by golfers." That statement is true for many of us because most of the time, we do not adequately prepare ourselves physically and mentally before we arrive at the first tee. All experienced golfers know that the first shot of the day often sets the tone for the rest of the round. Frequently, it can also determine whether you are going to play and score well that day. Perhaps you've witnessed–or even personally experienced–the golfer who...

...arrives at the golf course late, with no time to warm up or hit balls at the driving range;

...dashes to the first tee where other golfers have already teed off;

...fumbles through the golf bag for the driver, ball, tee, and glove–but cannot find the glove because it was left at home to dry, so has to borrow an ill-fitting one;

...holds breath to try to stop breathing rapidly–due to the rushing and irritation;

...takes two quick practice swings–and feels sharp pain in the back;

...slices the ball into the trees, a bunker or water hazard, and gets very irritated, even angry, loses his or her cool–and new ball;

...tries to make up for the bad drive by "killing" the ball with the next shot, and the ball goes 30 yards–about the same distance as the huge divot taken;

...swears–usually loudly–and gets even more upset;

...finally gets the ball on the green in four, and three-putts for a seven;

...blames everything–e.g., glove, course layout, condition–and everybody (but himself or herself) for the bad first hole score;

...gets to the second hole–still fuming–and holes out in six;

...after disastrous scores for five holes, scores first par.

These scenarios often occur because the golfer was not adequately prepared physically and mentally for the game!

You can get your round off to a good start by recognizing that you will need:

- Your 14 permitted golf clubs, cleaned and in good condition–and make sure you have the more important clubs. Your favorite driver, fairway wood or long iron, wedges, and putter will be the most used and therefore the most important clubs in your bag.
- At least six golf balls, more if you are playing a course that is unfamiliar, tight, or has a lot of water hazards.
- At least two good golf gloves in case one gets wet or torn.
- Prescriptions, if you are on medication for any medical problems, especially potentially life-threatening conditions like heart disease, high blood pressure, or diabetes. Be sure to keep adequate amounts of medication in your golf bag in case of an emergency.
- A pair of dry and comfortable golf shoes with no missing or badly worn-out spikes. Add special insoles (available at most good sports shops) into your shoes if you are overweight, or have foot or heel problems. Loosen the laces if your shoes are too tight because of the added insoles, or get bigger shoes.
- A light golf bag, if you are walking and carrying your own. Choose a bag with padded and comfortable straps. Double shoulder straps are easier on your back and shoulders than a single strap.
- The telephone number and a map to the golf course, if it is unfamiliar to you. Don't allow panic to set in should you get lost.
- A good night's sleep, and a clear schedule. Don't make appointments immediately before or after your round. No one can play well for more than a few holes if mentally or physically tired, or rushing to start or finish a game.
- A weather report. You don't want to forget your umbrella or rain suit if wet weather is a good possibility. Nor do you want to forget a sweater or jacket if the day is expected to be cold. It may be warm and dry in the city but cold, wet, and windy at a course on a mountain or next to the sea.

Additional suggestions on how to better prepare yourself mentally for your game are presented in Hole No. 9: Using Your Mind To Lower Your Golf Scores.

WHAT TO WEAR

- As a general rule, you're much better off to emphasize function over style when it comes to the type of golf clothing and shoes to wear.
- While it may be important to look good, it's more important to be comfortable.
- You have a better chance of playing well if your clothes and shoes are comfortable and not a concern.
- Choose light colored clothing, preferably 100% cotton, for warm or hot weather.
- Short-sleeved cotton shirts and short pants are best for hot-dry or hot-humid weather unless you need extra protection from the sun. Then, long-sleeved cotton shirts and long pants are recommended.
- For cooler weather, layers of clothing work best, especially as the temperature rises during the day and you need to shed some clothing as you and the weather get warmer.
- If rain is expected, bring along an umbrella, a water-proof jacket, suit or raincoat. Water-repellent windcheaters usually do not adequately prevent you from getting wet when it rains heavily.
- Ensure that your gloves, socks and shoes are dry and fit well. Wearing wet and uncomfortable ones over a 4- to 5-hour round of golf will help ruin your game.
- Choose shoes that are effectively waterproof if you are going to play on a wet course, very early in the morning when the dew is still present, or if rain is expected.
- If your clothes or socks get very wet from rain or excessive sweating, and you feel cold, change to dry ones as soon as possible, both for comfort and to prevent illness.

It is not essential to shower or have a bath immediately after a round of golf. However, do so as soon as it is convenient because you will feel more refreshed.

A warm shower or bath is usually more relaxing for most golfers than a cold one. My preference is to soak in a warm water jacuzzi or bathtub. Usually however, I just stand under a shower in a putting-like stance (back, hips, and knees slightly bent) with water, as hot as I can tolerate, spraying and relaxing my lower back muscles.

THE SKIN GAME–SKIN CARE

A healthy-looking tan may look good but it is neither healthy nor good for your skin and body. Prolonged and excessive exposure to sunlight and ultra-violet (UV) light can seriously damage your skin and is one of the causes of skin cancer. More than 300,000 new skin cancers occur in the United States every year. Some are very dangerous, while others are easily curable if treated early and adequately.

Our skin helps protect our bodies from bacterial invasion, prevents excess fluid loss, and regulates our temperature. Unfortunately, most golfers do not bother to care for their skin. If you want to prolong your golf days, you must start protecting your skin from further damage.

While most melanomas (mole cancers) can be cured with surgery, some cannot. Any mole or dark spot that grows rapidly, bleeds, itches, irritates, or changes color should be seen immediately by a physician.

The most common skin cancer among golfers is basal cell carcinoma. These cancers present as small, irregular, elevated, or nodular irritated spots that may bleed and itch. With continued growth, they involve surrounding tissues. Most basal cell carcinomas occur in yellow, irritated skin spots called keratoses, that can be caused by sunlight and removed to prevent later formation of such cancers.

Oiling your skin three or four times a day greatly helps in treating keratoses and some ointments can actually remove certain types of keratoses by killing the abnormal cells. Moisturizing soaps and bath lotions also help keep your skin soft and supple.

Exposure to sunlight can also cause cancer to the squamous cells of your lips. A lubrication stick with sunscreen should always be used when prolonged and excessive sun exposure is expected.

Fair-skinned blondes and redheads are more likely to develop skin cancers from sunlight or UV light, and therefore should take the most precautions. Naturally dark or deeply pigmented skins (not skins tanned by the sun or artificial UV light) are less likely to develop skin cancers, but adequate care should still be taken.

As plastic surgeon Dr. Charles E. Horton said in his Golf Digest article, *The Most Dangerous Skin Game:* "Golfers know the importance of slowing down the swing. It is, however even more important that we slow the sun damage to our bodies."

SKIN CARE TIPS

- Wear a hat, carry an umbrella, and if you are fair-skinned, consider wearing long-sleeved shirts and long pants.
- Consider playing in the early hours of the morning or the late hours of the afternoon.
- Whenever possible, avoid playing between 10:00 a.m. and 2:00 p.m. when the sun is usually most damaging, even on a cloudy day because UV light penetrates clouds.
- Wherever possible, park your motorized golf cart under a tree or shady area while waiting for your playing companion to play his or her shot.
- If you are on the fairway, park your motorized golf cart in a direction so that the sun does not shine on exposed parts of your body.
- If you carry your own bag or pull your own trolley cart, then you should walk or wait under trees or other shaded areas wherever possible.
- Use sun protection lip screen, and lotion or sunscreen on exposed parts of your head, neck, arms, and legs.
- Sunscreens should be used during prolonged exposure to sunlight, regardless of the temperature and whether the sun is shining brightly or not.
- Sunscreens should be applied in accordance with the manufacturer's instructions–liberally, repeatedly, and well in advance of exposure to the sun–preferably at least 15 minutes since they work better when there is enough time for them to be well-absorbed by your skin.
- This may also mean that before leaving for your game, applying them to your arms if they are exposed to the sun while you drive to the golf course.
- Use sunscreens that protect adequately against both ultra-violet A and B rays (UV-A and UV-B).
- A sunscreen with more than "15 SPF" (standardized sun protection factors) formula usually gives sufficient protection for most golfers.
- If your skin normally takes about ten minutes to burn after fairly continuous exposure to sunlight or UV light, then an SPF 15 sunscreen should protect you about 15 times longer–or about two and a half hours.
- As this time is usually sufficient only for about nine holes of golf, you should re-apply your sunscreen before starting the second nine if you are playing an 18-hole round. Therefore, a tube of sunscreen should be in your golf bag at all times.

- Alternatively, you should consider using sunscreens with higher SPF, especially if you are very fair-skinned, although SPF 30 may not give twice the protection of a SPF 15 sunscreen.
- It is not possible to recommend a single sunscreen for all golfers because of individual differences and preferences.
- Some golfers are allergic to PABA, the important ingredient in most sunscreens.
- Some creams have an alcohol base which may irritate the skin of other golfers, or may contain oils that make your skin slippery and allow the golf club to loosen in your grip.
- Golfers who sweat a lot should use waterproof sunscreens.
- Try to gradually expose your skin to the sun, avoiding excessive time in strong direct sunlight.
- Artificial tanning machines do not protect but merely cause your skin to brown. In fact, the tan ultimately leaves your skin, but the damage to the skin remains and with recurrent tanning, such damage may accumulate.
- You should also protect your eyes by using sunglasses that can protect from strong UV light and not only to reduce the intensity of light. In fact, many of the dark sunglasses offer less protection than the lighter glasses that are polarized.

Remember, should your skin become loose or wrinkled, a plastic surgeon may be able to tighten it. However, they cannot correct or undo the irreversible damage that you may cause to your skin because of prolonged and excessive exposure to sunlight and UV light without adequate protection and common sense care.

HOLE NO. 4

HEALTH PRECAUTIONS AND TIPS YOU SHOULD KNOW AS A GOLFER

> - If you are unfit, overweight, on medication, or have significant medical problems like heart disease, high blood pressure, or diabetes
> - The "FITT" formula exercise prescription

IF YOU ARE UNFIT, OVERWEIGHT, ON MEDICATION, OR HAVE SIGNIFICANT MEDICAL PROBLEMS LIKE HEART DISEASE, HIGH BLOOD PRESSURE, OR DIABETES

As discussed in Hole No. 1, golf is not a physically strenuous game, particularly when compared with more rigorous sports like basketball, tennis, and football. But, if you aren't having any fun and take the game way too seriously, it can become stressful physically and mentally. That makes it all the more important to monitor closely any medical problems that you may have.

If you have any significant medical problems or are on medication, you should consult your physician before playing golf. If you do not have a very serious medical problem, you need not be afraid your physician will stop you from playing golf–unless you consult one who is ignorant about the extensive benefits and minimal risks of low-level physical activities like golf. Very few medical conditions prohibit golf as an activity because in most cases you should be able to modify the way you play your golf to accommodate your current level of health and fitness. (Please refer to the end of Hole No. 6 for further information on "Should you stop playing golf when injured?")

Similarly, if you are on medication you should be able to continue playing golf in most instances, although you may have to be aware of the side effects of your medication that may prevent you from enjoying your round. *As an example, if you have heart disease or high blood pressure, and are on diuretics, you should drink more fluids because diuretics make your body produce and lose more water.* That is why you need to go to the restroom more often when you are taking these medication. The extra fluids you consume can help prevent dehydration, cramps, and other more serious complications.

As another example, if you are a diabetic going for a round of golf and are on insulin injection treatment, you should consider injecting yourself in areas other than your legs. This is particularly important if you intend to walk and carry your own bag or pull a trolley. The reason is that with the markedly increased blood flow in your legs and skin due to the exercise, there may be a higher rate of absorption of the injected insulin. This could result in attacks of hypoglycemia (low blood sugar) which can present as a feeling of weakness, faintness, trembling, or cold sweats. *Whether on insulin injection or tablet therapy, if you are a diabetic, you should ensure that you always have some candy bars and glucose tablets in your golf bag in case you need to quickly prevent or treat a hypoglycemic attack.*

If you have any significant medical problems, you should always inform at least one of your playing companions of your condition and where you keep your medication. This is so that should you suddenly develop any serious complications (e.g., lose consciousness from hypoglycemia, suffer a heart attack), someone can help you as much as possible without unnecessary delay. This may sometimes mean a difference between life and death.

There is nothing wrong with golf as exercise, especially if you walk and carry or pull your golf bag. But, let's face it, golf isn't the best way to get physically fit if you aren't already. The reason is that although walking is a very good way to get fit, during a round of golf, the walking is continuously interrupted. Becoming at least minimally fit will help you play better and enjoy your game more. But, if you are just starting the game and aren't in the best physical condition, it is suggested that you take things slowly, at least until you improve your fitness.

If you would like to start the habit of walking while you play golf, begin by playing nine holes or less, preferably on a shorter, flatter course. Put your golf bag on a pull cart, or carry just a few clubs, so that you get accustomed to the load. If you insist on playing 18 holes, start by walking nine holes or less, and riding in a motorized cart for the remaining holes. Or ask your cart partner if he or she minds if you walk every other hole.

If you really want to get into shape, the safest and most effective way to improve your health and fitness is through:

- A graduated aerobic exercise program, such as fairly continuous walking, stair-climbing, or cycling.
- A judicious diet which is especially important if you are overweight.

> ■ Adopting a healthier lifestyle, such as quitting smoking (or if that is not agreeable, then drastically cutting down on the amount of tobacco smoked or chewed), reducing your alcohol consumption, getting enough rest or sleep, and learning to better cope with the stress in your life.

THE "FITT" FORMULA EXERCISE PRESCRIPTION

The following "FITT" formula exercise prescription is in accordance with guidelines outlined recently by various medical and scientific organizations and individuals such as the American College of Sports Medicine, American Heart Association, the U.S. Centers for Disease Control and Prevention, the U.S. President's Council on Physical Fitness and Sports, the U.S. Surgeon General, and Kenneth H. Cooper, M.D., M.P.H. (founder of the Cooper Aerobics Center in Dallas, Texas, U.S.A., which includes the Cooper Clinic and the renowned Institute for Aerobics Research). If you do not have any significant medical problems and have a reasonable level of health and fitness, the following "FITT" formula guideline will ensure maximum benefits (particularly aerobic fitness) and minimum risks (e.g., cardiorespiratory, orthopedic, and heat stress problems):

F = Frequency of Exercise

Three to five times a week (on alternate days, if three times a week)

I = Intensity of Exercise

The intensity recommended by different authorities and experts for normal healthy adults ranges from about 60% to 90% of your actual or predicted maximum heart rate (MHR). However, based on Dr. Cooper's current health and longevity exercise program, 65% to 80% of MHR is sufficient for most golfers. Exercising past 80%, or in excess of frequency, type of activity, or duration recommended in this FITT formula, is acceptable only in healthy, fit persons who carefully listen to their bodies.

If you are starting an exercise program, you should not try too hard, too much, too soon. The reason is that you are more likely to develop muscle soreness, overstress, and overuse injuries. The end result is an increased chance of drop out or discontinuation of such participation in exercise programs.

High-intensity or prolonged activity would also result in excess free radicals. Dr. Cooper recommends that if you choose to exercise more rigorously, be sure to take extra antioxidant supplements for reasons explained in Hole No. 2: Your Golf Also Depends On What You Eat And Drink. For further details or information, please refer to more recent publications on free radicals, antioxidants, and exercise, particularly Dr. Cooper's *"The Antioxidant Revolution",* which is one of the recommended references listed at the end of this book.

The predicted MHR of a person is about 220 minus his or her age in years, with a variation of about 10 beats per minute (bpm).

Age (years)	MHR (bpm)	Heart Rates (in bpm) as % of Predicted MHR						
		60%	65%	70%	75%	80%	85%	90%
20	200	120	130	140	150	160	170	180
30	190	114	124	133	143	152	162	171
40	180	108	117	126	135	144	153	162
50	170	102	111	119	128	136	145	153
60	160	96	104	112	120	128	136	144

Using this table, you can check the intensity of your exercise by determining what your exercise heart rate is. To do so, you should have exercised for at least 3 to 5 minutes to allow your heart to adjust to the new exercise load. Then, stop your exercise–if possible for not more than about 15 to 20 seconds–and place your index and middle fingers (not thumb) gently against your heart or an artery–the most convenient arteries to feel are at your wrist, or the carotid arteries which are just to the right and left of your windpipe in the neck. (*Caution*: Do not press both right and left carotid arteries at the same time, or press even one carotid artery so firmly that you significantly reduce the blood flow to your brain as this may cause you to lose consciousness temporarily.)

To determine your heart rate (in bpm), look at the second hand on your watch and count the number of beats in:

6 seconds and multiply by 10,
or
10 seconds and multiply by 6.

By checking your heart rate while exercising, you will be able to find out fairly accurately just how hard you are working out–and whether you need to maintain, increase, or lower the intensity of your exercise.

Exercising fairly continuously for several minutes at the above recommended intensities usually means doing so until you begin to sweat and breathe deeply. However, you should not exercise until you become breathless, or develop any medical problems (e.g., giddiness, leg or chest pains).

As with all exercise activities, you should still be able to talk fairly normally while doing them. This is the so-called *"talk test."* If you cannot pass the talk test, then you are probably exercising harder than you are fit or ready for. Either slow down or introduce periodic short rests in your activity. For golf-fitness training, it is better to maintain fairly continuous activity. Therefore, slowing down is the better alternative. On the other hand, do not slow down so much that you do not exercise hard enough to gain sufficient benefit from the time and effort expended.

The best indications that you are working at a beneficial, yet safe level are:

- Being able to continue to talk fairly normally.
- Feeling slightly warm and even working up a little sweat.
- Breathing slightly faster and deeper than normal without becoming breathless, uncomfortable, or developing any medical problem (e.g. chest or leg pain, giddiness).
- A heart rate that is at least several beats above your normal resting rate (minimally about 10 to 20 beats above, and ideally about 30 to 60 beats above resting heart rate).

T = Type of Activity

A combination of aerobic, stretching, and calisthenic exercises. The actual choice of activities should depend on your preferred interest, current level of health and fitness, availability of facilities, and skill ability (particularly for racket games and ball games).

T = Time Duration

20 to 60 minutes of fairly continuous aerobic exercise during each session. There should also be at least three to five minutes of warm-up aerobic and stretching exercises before, and another three to five minutes of cool-down stretching exercises, after the aerobic exercises.

If you are a non-competitive athlete, studies have shown that exercising beyond the recommended limits may not significantly increase the benefits. On the other hand, your risk of developing medical problems, especially injuries, may be significantly increased. For effective reduction of excess body fat, you must use up at least 200 to 300 kilocalories during each exercise session. This can be met by the minimum requirements provided in the above "FITT" formula.

If you are trying to ease into shape when you are overweight, have been physically inactive for some time, are very unfit, or have significant medical problems, the "FITT" formula guideline should be modified through an interplay between the frequency, intensity, time duration, and type of activities permissible. Such amended exercise prescriptions should, wherever possible, be under the supervision of your physician. For example, if you are very unfit (e.g., have uncomplicated cardiorespiratory problems), you may initially have to be restricted to the following amended "FITT" formula guideline:

F = Frequency   : Several times daily.

I =   Intensity   : Very low (e.g., less than 60% of safe maximum functional heart rate).

T = Type of activity   : Slow, level walking for short distances and light stretches or calisthenics.

T = Time duration   : Less than 20 minutes of light aerobic or calisthenic exercises.

> ■ Slow down or stop exercising if significant signs and symptoms (e.g., chest pains, breathlessness) develop. If you begin such a modified exercise program and have good results–feel better and stronger, and if your health problems seem to be less severe–then it is all right to step up your workout routine. Don't be afraid to do more exercise, but always remember to check with your physician before making any *major* increases in your exercise load. Slow down or stop your exercise if you feel any discomfort or pain. This is to enable further improvements to be achieved, while still minimizing the possible risks involved.
>
> ■ Choose an exercise program that is sufficiently beneficial, safe, and appropriate to your needs as well as to your health and fitness status. Always begin slowly and gradually build up to your desired or required amount of exercise.

- ***Remember to "train, but not overstrain."*** Please refer to Hole No. 7 for more information on which aerobic exercise programs (e.g., walking, bicycling, stair-climbing, step-ups, or jogging) are most suitable, safest, convenient, and enjoyable for you.

- Four to six weeks of a low-level and gradual conditioning program of mild to moderate physical activities (e.g., walking, light stretches, or calisthenics) are recommended for everyone before more rigorous activities (e.g., jogging, aerobic dancing, tennis and other racket or ball games) are undertaken. This is particularly important if you are very unfit or are over 40 years of age.

- Do not exercise when you are ill or suffering from a significant medical problem, including injury or acute infection (e.g., viral flu or chest infection). Serious complications may result. Resume only when you have fully recovered and then ensure that you gradually build up to your previously desired or required amount of exercise. Consult your physician for advice, if necessary.

- Avoid the extremes of heat or cold of the day whenever possible. Do not exercise in extreme heat or cold unless you are well acclimatized and sufficiently fit to withstand the added stress. Especially under hot and humid conditions, make sure you reduce your chances of developing heat stress disorders or problems (e.g., heat cramps, exhaustion, and stroke). You should do so by drinking as much fluids as you can and wearing the correct clothing. If necessary, add a small amount of electrolytes, like a pinch of table salt, to replace those lost in your sweat, especially in the first days of exposure to increased heat or humidity.

- High humidity is often more important than high temperature as a contributor to heat stress problems. That is why it is possible to develop such problems at relatively low temperatures (e.g., 80 to 85 degrees F) when the humidity is high.

- Fluids should be taken before, during, and after exercise. In an environment of high temperature and humidity, it is particularly important that the increased body temperature generated during exercise be reduced rapidly, by enabling the sweat produced to be evaporated quickly. It is therefore advisable that you exercise in shorts and T-shirts rather than long pants, long-sleeved shirts, or warm-up suits.

- Allow the blood in your legs to flow freely back to your heart by not standing or sitting still immediately after rigorous exercise. Failure to do so may result in giddiness, fainting, or more serious complications. Cool down slowly by walking for at least three to five minutes.

- If you are very tired, lie on your back with your head flat on the surface and your feet raised about 6 to 12 inches above the level of your head.

- Should you injure yourself, or if pain develops in the course of your exercise, slow down or stop completely if necessary. ***Never exercise beyond pain limits.*** Follow the "RICE" treatment for all minor golf injuries as outlined in Hole No. 6.

- Exercising rigorously only once a week may be more of a hazard than a help, particularly for those who are very unfit. This is because the body has been deconditioned for six days, and by the seventh day, would probably lack the fitness for rigorous exercise. Yet it is expected to perform like a very fit body. The risk of developing medical problems will expectedly be much higher.

- Exercise helps improve health and fitness, but only if done regularly. Recent studies have shown that these exercises need not be rigorous or prolonged. Just walking as much as you can in your daily life (e.g., by not taking the elevator or escalator) has been shown to be beneficial.

- ***Furthermore, the risk of developing medical problems if you exercise properly are usually few and minor. On the other hand, the risk of developing serious medical problems is much greater if you continue to be physically inactive.*** Examples of such medical problems are coronary artery disease, high blood pressure, diabetes, obesity, and lower back problems including "slipped discs."

32

HOLE NO. 5

EXERCISES YOU SHOULD DO JUST BEFORE, DURING, AND AFTER GOLF

- The recommended warm-up exercises
- Simple, safe, and effective stretching exercises which can be done at the golf course

THE RECOMMENDED WARM-UP EXERCISES

In an ideal world, all golfers would spend at least 30 minutes doing 30 or more exercises to stretch all the muscles and ligaments involved in the golf swing–before they take their first swing or hit their first ball at the practice range or first tee. Still in our ideal world, golfers would then spend at least 30 minutes hitting balls with gradually increasing swing speed and power on the practice tee before beginning their round. However, most recreational golfers won't find the time nor the discipline to do 30 exercises or warm up the correct way at the practice tee before playing a round of golf.

Golfers are particularly disinterested in doing exercises, especially if they have to spend several minutes doing more than a few simple exercises before their round of golf. Most would much rather spend the time it would take to exercise, hitting golf balls on the practice tee, or rolling putts on the putting green. Professional golfers and accomplished amateurs know better. They realize it is equally important to have muscles and ligaments that are adequately warmed up and stretched even *before* hitting the first ball at the practice range or the first tee. This is because such muscles and ligaments are stronger, function more efficiently, and less likely to be injured.

Based on my personal experiences, another reason for not trying to teach golfers too many exercises at once is because it can be a waste of time and effort. Only the exceptional golfer will do all the exercises before the start of his or her round of golf. Many will try a few, and a great many others won't try any at all because they think that if they can't do them all, it is useless to even do just a few!

Therefore, in this chapter I will only present those pre-game exercises which are simple, convenient, take only a few minutes, safe, and considered the more important ones from recent research, and from my professional and personal experiences with thousands of golfers over the past 20 years. Golfers who want information on additional exercises to get fitter and healthier should refer to Hole No. 7: Golf-Fitness Exercises You Can

Easily Do At Home, Workplace, or Travel, and Hole No. 8: Exercises You Can Do To Prevent Or Treat Common Golf Injuries.

Warming Up

The two most important principles when exercising to improve health, fitness, performance, and prevent injuries are the principles of gradual overload and specificity. This means gradually increasing the load, resistance, or intensity (but always within pain-free limits) on each muscle, ligament, joint, and movement that is specifically used in that sport, game or activity. More recent medical and scientific studies have also shown that it is more effective and safer if the muscles and ligaments are adequately warmed up *before* they are stretched. The reason is that with the increased blood flow and temperature, they are more efficient and less likely to be injured.

The most effective way to warm up the body and most of the muscles, ligaments, and joints used in golf is to exercise the large muscles in your lower limbs. For golfers preparing for a round of golf, the simplest warm-up for the body is to walk. You should walk briskly (preferably with your arms pumping) and fairly continuously for at least three to five minutes–10 to 20 minutes is even better. If this is inconvenient, or you're embarrassed to have your friends see you walking briskly around the parking lot or other areas near the golf course, try climbing stairs in the clubhouse. Or you can find some remote area of the clubhouse or locker room and do some walking or running in place for a few minutes. This warm-up procedure can be accelerated by wearing warm clothing when it is cold.

The point is to warm up adequately for your golf without getting tired, becoming breathless, or sweating profusely. *Therefore you need only get your heart rate to somewhere around 10 to 30 beats above your resting heart rate (which is about 45% to 55% of your maximum heart rate) as this would usually be sufficient for most golfers.* Although the terror of the first tee may get your heart pounding harder than normal, this is usually not sufficient to warm up the muscles and ligaments of your body, increase their blood flow, improve their efficiency, and to help you play better. If a simple warm-up walk, stair-climb, or running in place causes you to breathe too hard or sweat too much, you are probably trying too hard or are badly out of shape, and need to start a regular exercise and diet program. Older or less fit golfers are also more likely to experience such a situation after a few holes of golf or walking up a slope. That is why they usually play better golf when they lose their excess fat through judicious dieting, and improve their health and fitness through a healthier lifestyle, especially correct and regular exercise.

Unlike athletes in more rigorous sports and games, it is not necessary for golfers to warm up so much that they begin to sweat continuously or profusely. This is usually equivalent to at least 40 to 60 beats above a person's resting heart rate or 60% to 70% of maximum heart rate. It is very unlikely that a golfer with such a pounding heart and who is breathing heavily and sweating profusely, will be able to play good golf.

Before You Start

After at least three to five minutes of warm-up exercises, you can begin some stretching exercises, but you must remember some important points:

- **Warm up sufficiently**–for the reasons mentioned above.
- **Breathe normally**–be certain you breathe normally while doing these exercises. That may sound obvious, but many people hold their breath while doing some exercises. This isn't recommended as you need the oxygen from normal breathing for your body to function efficiently.
- **Be on guard for pain**–it is your body's natural protective mechanism to tell you that it is not ready or able to exercise past this limit. Therefore, always do all warm-up and stretching exercises within pain-free limits. Slowly stretch until you feel some strain (but no actual physical pain).
- **Count and hold**–stay in the stretching position for 10 to 15 seconds without jerking or bouncing. (**Tip**: When counting to hold for 10 seconds, say "thousand and one, thousand and two.....", until you reach "thousand and ten". If you say "1, 2, 3, 4, 5, 6, 7, 8, 9, 10", you would probably only be holding for about five to eight seconds).
- **Start position may differ**–unless otherwise indicated, if you are sitting or standing, you should be relaxed with your arms by your sides and your feet about shoulder-width apart. If you are lying on your back, then your arms should be by your sides and knees bent about 90 degrees.
- **Return to start position**–do so slowly and gradually after the completion of each exercise.
- **Repeat each exercise three to five times**–unless otherwise indicated, it would be ideal if you do each exercise at least three to five times, gradually increasing the time duration and degree of stretch for each major group of muscle and ligament used in golf.

SIMPLE, SAFE, AND EFFECTIVE STRETCHING EXERCISES WHICH CAN BE DONE AT THE GOLF COURSE

Remember that golf involves your whole body and you should warm up and stretch all major parts of your body adequately before you hit your first ball at the practice range or first tee. The following stretching exercises are presented in order of head and neck, shoulders and upper limbs, upper and lower back, hips and lower limbs. This is because you are less likely to forget to do the more important stretches for all the major parts of your body if you do them in this order.

Head, Neck, and Shoulder Exercises

Caution: If you have head, neck, or cervical spine problems, it is not advisable to do any neck exercises without first consulting your physician. Circular or semicircular neck rotation exercises and those done until you feel a click, or can feel or hear sounds from your neck joints, are also not advisable. Such exercises may cause injury, or make you feel giddy or faint. Should you develop such problems, or have any pain, tingling, or numbing sensations down your arms while doing the following recommended exercises, reduce your range of stretch. If the symptoms persist, stop your exercise. If you feel giddy or faint, you should lie down with your head flat on the ground or a bench, and your feet raised about 6 to 12 inches. Breathe normally and stay in this position until you have fully recovered.

Neck Extension Exercise

Relax in a sitting or standing position. With a thumb pushing chin upward, slowly tilt head upward until you feel stretch (but no pain) at front of neck and spine. Hold position for 10 to 15 seconds while breathing normally.

Neck Flexion Exercise

Relax in a sitting or standing position. With hands clasped behind head, slowly tilt head downward to try to touch chin against chest until you feel stretch (but no pain) at the back of neck and spine. Hold position for 10 to 15 seconds while breathing normally.

Neck Rotation Exercises

Relax in a sitting or standing position. With right fingers gently pushing jaw, slowly rotate neck horizontally to look as far left as possible until you feel stretch (but no pain) at side of neck and spine. Hold position for 10 to 15 seconds while breathing normally. Repeat this exercise for other side.

Neck Side Tilting Exercises

Relax in a sitting or standing position. With left hand on right side of head, slowly tilt head toward left shoulder until you feel a stretch (but no pain) at side of neck and spine. Hold position for 10 to 15 seconds while breathing normally. Repeat exercise for other side.

Shoulder Stretching Exercises

Relax in a sitting or standing position. With left hand, slowly pull right elbow across chest and toward left shoulder until you feel stretch (but no pain) on outside of right shoulder. Hold position for 10 to 15 seconds while breathing normally. Repeat exercise for left shoulder.

Wrist and Forearm Exercises

The following recommended pre-game exercises are simple and effective in stretching your finger and wrist flexor and extensor muscles and tendons which originate from your elbow. Injuries to these tendons at your elbow are the causes of "golfer's elbow" (on the inner side of elbow) and "tennis elbow" (on the outer side of elbow), both of which are common among golfers. This is especially so for those with forearm muscles that are weak or tight (because they are not adequately stretched before the first golf ball is hit at the practice range or first tee).

Wrist Rotation Exercises

Relax in a sitting or standing position. Keep both elbows fairly straight but relaxed by your sides. Slowly rotate both wrists in a circular and clockwise direction for 10 to 15 seconds, then anti-clockwise direction for 10 to 15 seconds, while breathing normally.

Bring one arm up to a horizontal position in front of you with palm facing the ground. Keep elbow fairly straight and relaxed. This is the neutral position for the next four exercises.

Wrist Flexor and Forearm Extensor Muscle Exercises

With left hand holding right fingers, bend right wrist downward until you feel a stretch in right wrist, finger and wrist extensor muscles on upper side of forearm. Hold position for 10 to 15 seconds while breathing normally.

Wrist Extensor and Forearm Flexor Muscle Exercises

With left hand holding right fingers, bend right wrist upward until you feel a stretch in right wrist, finger and wrist flexor muscles on the lower side of the forearm. Hold position for 10 to 15 seconds while breathing normally.

Tip: It is recommended that you do these stretching exercises separately and in turn as described. However, if you arrive at the golf course late and have insufficient time to do all these exercises even once before teeing off, it is possible to save some time by doing some of them together–for example, do your right and left wrist flexor exercises at the same time, or your wrist exercises together with the shoulder stretch.

Lower Back and Spine Exercises

Caution: If you have back or spine problems, it is not advisable to do any back exercises without first consulting your physician. If you feel any pain, tingling, or numbing sensations running down your legs while doing the following recommended exercises, reduce on your range of stretch. If the symptoms persist, stop your exercise.

Anyone who has experienced back problems as I have–just like about 80% of people would some time in their life–can tell you how painful and debilitating they can be. Therefore, it is essential that you take care of your back by remembering and doing a few simple precautionary measures that will help you avoid such problems. A bad back will, among other things, keep you off the golf course for an extended period of time. No golfer wants that.

As mentioned in the Introduction, during a golf trip in 1990, I suffered a severe "slipped" disc in the lower back–with sciatica–after carrying a golf bag and suitcase which were too heavy for me. After refusing surgery as the first treatment option, I treated myself with judicious rest, medication, and very intensive stretching and strengthening back exercises. Within three months, I recovered sufficiently to resume playing competitive golf. Since then, I have been even more conscious of the need to avoid activities that may cause or aggravate lower back problems. I also continue to do the recommended exercises regularly to strengthen and stretch the muscles and ligaments of the lower back. You should do your back exercises just before, during and immediately after a round of golf or other physical activities (e.g., gardening).

It is not advisable to bend your back forward in a standing position with your knees straight. This is because many studies have shown that this puts excessive stress and strain on the muscles, ligaments, and joints in your lumbar-sacral spine and may cause or aggravate lower back problems, including "slipped" discs. If you must bend your back forward in the standing position, then you should keep your knees slightly bent, preferably with one foot in front of the other as shown in Hole No. 8.

It is best to do lower back exercises in the lying position. However, just before, during, and after your round of golf, it is not easy to find suitable places at the golf course to lie down to do exercises.

Therefore, for these practical reasons, I recommend that the following exercises in the sitting position be done as a good alternative because they are simple, yet safe and sufficiently effective. You can sit on a golf cart, the rear end of a station-wagon, bench, chair, step, cartpath curb, wheel of your trolley, car seat, or any other raised structure that would allow you to sit comfortably with your hips and knees bent about 90^{0} and feet about shoulder-width apart (the neutral sitting position for the next four exercises).

Warm-up and stretching exercises should be done before, during, and after a round of golf. However, they are particularly important when the weather is cold and rainy.

Back Strengthening Exercise in the Sitting Position

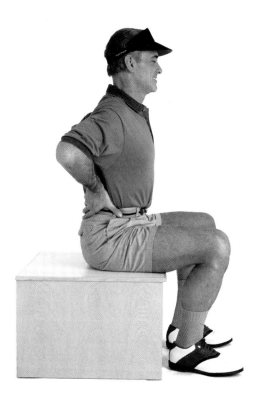

From neutral sitting position, with hands on lower back muscles, slowly push lower back forward with hands and by gradual contraction of lower back muscles. This should make you sit fairly upright, and you should feel a contraction and stretch (but no pain) in your lower back. Hold position for 10 to 15 seconds while breathing normally. Relax back to the neutral sitting position.

Forward Bending Lower Back Stretching Exercise in the Sitting Position

From neutral sitting position, slowly bend head and body forward until you feel a stretch in lower back. Hold position for 10 to 15 seconds while breathing normally. Relax to the neutral sitting position. *Tip*: It is easier to hold position at the maximum stretch if you wrap your arms around the calf muscles and pull your body toward the thighs.

Side Rotation Lower Back Stretching Exercise in the Sitting Position

From neutral sitting position, with right hand on lower back, hold outside of right knee with left hand. Slowly rotate head, shoulders, and body to right with help of left hand pull. You should feel stretch (but no pain) at sides of body. Hold position for 10 to 15 seconds while breathing normally. Repeat this exercise for other side.

Side Rotation Lower Back Stretching Exercise in the Sitting Position

When you are fit enough and want a greater rotation stretch, bend body forward while rotating.

Lower Limb Exercises

Quadriceps Muscle and Knee Stretching Exercise

Stand and balance with right hand holding golf cart, bench, chair, or other sturdy object. Bend left knee and hold front of left ankle with left hand, and gently pull heel upward and backward until you feel stretch in left knee and quadriceps. Hold position for 10 to 15 seconds while breathing normally. Repeat exercise for right leg.

Hamstring Muscle Stretching Exercise in the Sitting Position

Sit with left hip and knee joints bent slightly more than 90°, with both hands clasped around the back of left thigh. Keeping left hip bent and hands behind left thigh, slowly try to straighten left knee by bringing left foot upward, until you feel stretch in left hamstrings. Hold position for 10 to 15 seconds while breathing normally. Repeat this stretching exercise for right hamstring muscles.

Note: I prefer this hamstring stretching exercise in the sitting position rather than the more commonly recommended "hurdle" sitting position or standing position, with one leg raised to hip level. My personal experience is that this sitting hamstring stretch is easier to control, and there is less stress on my lower back, hips, and knees. Therefore, it is safer, yet just as effective, especially for the less fit, the older golfers, and those with lower back, hip, or knee problems.

Calf Muscle, Achilles Tendon and Ankle Stretching Exercise in the Sitting Position

In the sitting position, straighten both knees. Slowly bring both ankles back until you feel stretch (but no pain) in calf muscles and Achilles tendons. Hold position for 10 to 15 seconds while breathing normally. Gradually return feet to the ground.

Note: I prefer this stretching exercise in the sitting position rather than the more commonly recommended standing position, stretching one or both sides together, because it is easier to control the stretch in this sitting position and therefore safer, yet equally effective.

Ankle Dorsiflexor Muscle and Ankle Stretching Exercises in the Sitting Position

In a relaxed sitting position, straighten both knees and slowly point toes by bending both ankles away from you until you feel stretch (but no pain) in the front muscles of leg and front of ankles. Hold position for 10 to 15 seconds while breathing normally. Gradually return feet to the ground.

HOLE NO. 6

HOW TO TREAT YOUR INJURIES ON OR OFF THE GOLF COURSE

- The "RICE" first aid treatment
- The benefits and dangers of common medications used to treat golf injuries
- Do you have to stop playing golf when injured?

THE "RICE" FIRST AID TREATMENT

If you play a lot of golf, especially as you get older, and neglect your fitness, injuries are usually inevitable. From tendinitis to "slipped" discs, your range of golf-related maladies can be quite wide. The management of golf injuries consists of prevention, treatment, and rehabilitation. In Hole No. 5, we discussed the best way to prevent injuries–proper warm-up, a stretching routine, cool-down exercises, and strengthening exercises. In this chapter, we will only discuss the principles of first aid treatment and the treatment of golf injuries with medication and exercises. The more specific prevention and treatment of common golf injuries will be addressed in Hole No. 8.

"RICE" is an acronym for **R**est, **I**ce, **C**ompression and **E**levation. These are most often recommended for the immediate care and treatment of minor golf injuries such as contusions, hematomas, sprains, strains and muscle pulls. If you are not sure about the nature and severity of your injury, talk to your physician before using the "RICE" treatment. The following "RICE" treatment procedure is recommended, especially in the first two to four days after injury:

Rest the injured part and dress any wounds present with sterile or antiseptic dressings. Resting or immobilizing the injured part will help avoid aggravating the injury, reduce pain and prevent greater inflammatory changes.

Ice or cold pack is to be applied to the injured part and immediate surrounding areas for 20 to 30 minutes and repeated about every three hours if necessary. (See next sections for more details regarding ice or cold pack treatment.)

Compression bandage around the injured part for at least two days particularly if there is bleeding or swelling.

Elevate or raise the injured part above the level of your heart, particularly if there is bleeding and swelling. Elevation reduces pressure in the tissues, and helps drain away collected fluids, thereby helping to reduce swelling, congestion of blood, and pain in the injured parts.

Do not massage the injured parts or apply any form of heat on the first day of injury. Both these procedures may aggravate your injury through increased swelling, bleeding (especially with rough massaging), and delay healing.

Ice or Cold Pack Treatment

For this treatment to be effective, it must be administered for more than ten minutes continuously. Anything less will usually not be sufficiently effective in reducing your pain or inflammation. However, cold treatment can be quite uncomfortable at first.

The following sensations are usually felt by most people:

■ First three minutes—a "cold" sensation.
■ Next five minutes—a "burning" sensation.
■ Next two minutes—an "aching" sensation.
■ After ten minutes—numbness and decrease in pain.

Types of Ice or Cold Pack Treatment

■ Crushed ice cubes in a plastic bag are most easily available on the golf course or club house. *Always carry at least one plastic bag and a compression bandage in your golf bag.*
■ Re-usable synthetic cold packs are available at most pharmacies. Keep them in your home freezer so that they are always available for immediate use.
■ Towels soaked in ice water or soaking the injured part (e.g., a finger) in ice water.
■ Most instant, non-reusable chemical cold packs are expensive and not very effective.
■ Cold sprays (e.g., ethyl chloride) should be used only by medical or paramedical personnel (e.g., physicians, physical therapists, trainers) who have been specially trained in their use. Such sprays should never be used near your eyes or on open wounds.

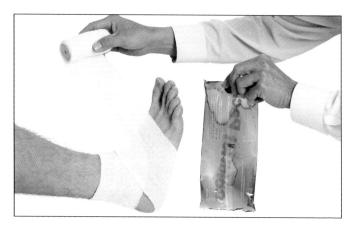

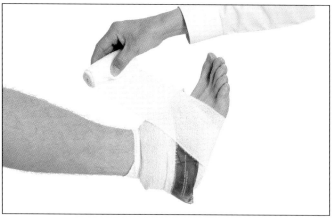

- Apply the ice or cold pack over the injured part using a compression bandage. The bandage should cover the injured area and a few inches above and below it. If a cold pack is not available, use broken-up ice cubes in a plastic bag instead.
- To reduce the discomfort, cover the injured area with one layer of the bandage, a clean handkerchief, or a thin towel before applying the pack. The cold penetration will then be more gradual and helps reduce your chances of frost-bite to the skin.
- Do not wrap the bandage so tightly that it cuts off circulation to the injured part and causes the areas to be pale, numb, or blue.
- Compression, like ice, helps reduce swelling, bleeding, bruising, and provides pain relief by supporting your injured muscles, tendons, ligaments, and joints.
- If you have vascular disease or diabetes, check with your physician before using an elastic bandage. If wrapped too tightly, it can interfere with your blood circulation and cause complications.

Some Possible Contra-indications to Ice or Cold Pack Treatment

■ Cold allergy–an itch or skin rash after cold treatment.
■ Frost-bite.
■ Thrombosis or blood clots in blood vessels.
■ Local blood circulatory disorders–especially among heavy smokers (e.g., Raynaud's phenomenon, Buerger's disease).

THE BENEFITS AND DANGERS OF COMMON MEDICATIONS USED TO TREAT GOLF INJURIES

Most minor injuries can be treated with analgesics, which are medications that relieve pain. Examples of analgesics include acetaminophen and non-steroidal anti-inflammatory drugs (NSAIDs) such as aspirin, ibuprofen and naproxen. NSAIDs relieve pain, and other signs and symptoms of inflammation such as swelling, redness, warmth, and loss of function. These are often important factors even in minor golf injuries because they may prevent the golfer from playing well or just getting onto the course. NSAIDs are called "non-steroidal" to distinguish them from corticosteroid drugs, such as cortisone, which also relieve pain and reduce inflammation.

When you are not sure what and how severe your injury is, or if your injury is worse, or if there is no improvement after a day or two, it is strongly recommended that you see your physician. Your physician may prescribe a mild analgesic drug to reduce your pain, or an NSAID to relieve both pain and inflammation. In some cases, he or she may recommend an injection of a corticosteroid drug directly into the injured area to help reduce pain and inflammation. Do not combine medication unless directed to do so by your physician.

Acetaminophen

This analgesic relieves pain but not the other signs and symptoms of inflammation. Therefore, it does not reduce swelling or stiffness in injured tissues, and is effective only for minor aches and pains. Acetaminophen is available in name-brand and generic forms without a prescription. It does not usually irritate your stomach or cause bleeding problems, and is often a good choice if you cannot use aspirin or other NSAIDs. However, if you drink large amounts of alcohol or have liver or kidney disorders, you should avoid taking acetaminophen because some side-effects have been reported. This is because an overdose or prolonged use of acetaminophen, especially in combination with alcohol, can cause severe liver or kidney damage.

Non-steroidal Anti-inflammatory Drugs (NSAIDs)

NSAIDs such as aspirin, ibuprofen and naproxen are commonly used to relieve pain, reduce stiffness and swelling in injured muscles, ligaments and joints. When you damage tissues during an injury, your body automatically responds by producing substances called prostaglandins. They cause large numbers of white blood cells and fluids to accumulate in the damaged tissue resulting in swelling and inflammation. Prostaglandins also stimulate pain-sensitive nerve cells in your injured tissues to send signals along nerve pathways to your brain, where your pain is actually felt.

NSAIDs work by blocking production of prostaglandins. They also inhibit the activity of your white blood cells, thereby reducing swelling and inflammation. NSAIDs prevent stimulation of pain-sensitive nerve cells so that the pain signals cannot get to your brain. Various name-brand and generic NSAIDs may be purchased without a prescription. The effectiveness and ability to tolerate a specific NSAID varies from golfer to golfer. Therefore, you are advised to ask your physician which type of NSAID is best for you, especially if you have a recurrent problem and need long-term or repeated medication. NSAIDs can cause stomach irritation and bleeding, especially when your stomach is empty, so always take them with food.

Tip: I prefer to take my NSAIDs at the start of a meal because I am assured that the food that I eat will push the tablet down into the stomach. If you take your tablet at the end of your meal, you must ensure that you drink enough fluids otherwise the tablet may sometimes get stuck in your esophagus, causing irritation. Furthermore, when it finally gets to your stomach, there may be little or no food present, and you are more likely to develop gastric irritation.

Golfers who have peptic ulcers, bleeding disorders, liver, or kidney disease, those on anti-coagulant medication, and women golfers who are pregnant or breast-feeding, should not take NSAIDs without clearance from their physician. The chances of side effects from NSAIDs, especially damage to your kidneys, increase as you get older. If you are over 50, you are advised to talk to your physician before taking NSAIDs. Also, do not give aspirin (acetyl salicylic acid) to your children if they are ill with a fever because aspirin has been linked with Reye's syndrome, a potentially fatal condition.

For treatment of acute but minor golf injuries, NSAIDs need be taken only for a few days (usually less than one week). For chronic and more serious injuries, you should see a physician who may prescribe NSAIDs for two weeks or even more.

Corticosteroid Drugs and Medication

Corticosteroid hormones are produced by our body's adrenal glands and are important for the proper functioning of our immune system (the body's natural defenses against infection) and the regulation of our metabolism (the biochemical processes that take place in our body). Corticosteroid drugs, such as cortisone, imitate the actions of corticosteroid hormones in our body. These drugs are used mainly for their very strong anti-inflammatory effect. They inhibit the activity of our white blood cells and block production of prostaglandins. This means that corticosteroids very effectively reduce pain, and the other signs and symptoms of inflammation.

Corticosteroids are available only with a prescription and are often used to treat pain and inflammation in those who do not respond to NSAIDs or other medication. Sometimes, corticosteroid drugs are injected directly into a joint or around a tendon to relieve inflammation caused by an injury that is healing slowly. Because corticosteroids can cause peptic ulcers, they should not be taken by golfers who are being treated for such a condition. Because they suppress our immune system, corticosteroids are not advisable for people who have, or are at risk of developing serious infections.

Anabolic Steroid Drugs ("Steroids")

Anabolic steroid drugs (commonly called "steroids", and often confused with corticosteroids) are synthetic bodybuilding hormones that can help increase muscle bulk, strength, and body growth. They are extremely dangerous drugs that imitate the actions of the male sex hormone, testosterone. Use of anabolic steroids by athletes is widely criticized by physicians, and prohibited by most sports authorities and athletic organizations around the world for ethical reasons, and because of the serious, potentially life-threatening health risks.

The possible health risks include acne, baldness, fluid retention, hardening of arteries, damage to your adrenal glands, damage to the testicles, infertility, impotence, liver damage, certain types of cancer, and death. In addition to the adverse effects listed above, adolescent males who take anabolic steroids also risk impairing the normal development of their muscles and bones, resulting in stunted growth.

Muscle Relaxants and Enzyme Preparations

Muscle relaxants are useful in golf injuries where there is significant muscle spasm. They relieve pain by reducing muscle spasm and allow you to be more mobile. Enzyme preparation tablets can be very effective in helping to reduce swelling (e.g., contusions, hematomas). They are usually given for three to five days, if your injury is not a serious one.

Creams, Ointments and Other Topical Medications

The types of topical medications that can be used in treating golf injuries are anti-inflammatories, counter-irritants, or cold sprays. Anti-inflammatory creams and ointments are useful especially for the more superficial and milder golf injuries (e.g., contusions), and when you are unable to tolerate oral NSAIDs. For deeper-seated injuries (e.g., knee joint injuries), their effectiveness would naturally be very limited.

Counter-irritant creams, ointments, and lotions produce "warmth" or a "cooling" effect so that your brain feels the "irritation" on your skin rather than feel the pain from your injury. They are also used during warm-ups by some athletes. Cold sprays such as ethyl chloride sprays, provide cooling of your skin and underlying tissues. It helps reduce pain as a form of cold (or ice) treatment as well as a counter-irritant.

Injections

With the availability of effective oral analgesics and NSAIDs now, injections are not as commonly used in the treatment of golf injuries as before. One of the most commonly used injections contains a corticosteroid (to reduce inflammation), local anesthetic (for pain relief) and an enzyme (to help disperse the corticosteroid). This "cocktail" can be used in the treatment of some very chronic golf injuries involving ligaments or tendons (such as "golfer's elbow" and "tennis elbow").

However, extreme care must be taken with such steroid injections, and a period of complete rest and abstinence from golf (usually for at least two to three weeks) should be enforced. After that, gradual strengthening exercises must be started prior to resuming golf or any other physical activity that requires some degree of stress on the injected injured structure. Failure to comply with these requirements may result in an aggravation of your injury from a partial tear to a severe tear or even complete rupture of the muscle, tendon, or ligament. The reason is that after the injection, the golfer may not feel significant pain (because of the very strong anti-inflammatory effect) and thinking that the injury has recovered sufficiently, goes out and stresses the tissue and causes greater damage.

DO YOU HAVE TO STOP PLAYING GOLF WHEN INJURED?

The simple answer to this question is very rarely–provided you listen carefully to your physician and your body (e.g., never playing or exercising until you feel pain as it is your body's protective mechanism to tell you that you are not fit or ready for that type or intensity of activity). You must accept the fact that when you are injured or have other significant medical problems, your body will be weaker than usual–so you should modify your golf game accordingly.

As mentioned in Hole No. 4, *if you have any significant medical problems, serious injuries, or are on medication, you should consult your physician before starting or continuing to playing golf.* If you do not have a very serious problem, you need not be afraid your physician will stop you from playing golf–unless you consult one who is ignorant about the extensive benefits and minimal risks of low-level physical activities like golf. Very few medical conditions or injuries prohibit golf as an activity. In most cases you should be able to modify the way you play your golf to accommodate your current level of health and fitness. If this reduction in frequency, intensity, time duration or type of activity, still causes pain or discomfort, you must stop your golf until you have recovered sufficiently.

As a sports medicine physician of 20 years, I have learned that regular exercisers are very reluctant to stop their activities. Golfers are among the most difficult persons to persuade to stop their activity–even for a week or two–because of their passion for the game, and since most feel that their injuries are not so serious as to warrant total stoppage–and rightly so! It is not possible to list all injuries and medical conditions that require you to stop playing golf temporarily until you recover sufficiently.

The following are some of the more common ones:

- Recent fractures, dislocations, or other serious injuries that have not healed sufficiently.
- Recent serious lower back injuries like a "slipped" disc, particularly when it is associated with neurological problems like sciatica (numbness, weakness, tingling sensations running down the back of your thighs and legs).
- Serious heart or lung diseases (e.g., heart attack, emphysema).
- Acute and severe viral or bacterial infections particularly when associated with a high fever–like a bad flu. Viral infections may cause viral myocarditis–inflammation of the heart muscle which may then be so weak that it may fail and result in serious complications including death.

HOLE NO. 7

GOLF-FITNESS EXERCISES YOU CAN EASILY DO AT HOME, WORKPLACE, OR TRAVEL

- What is a simple, safe, yet beneficial and enjoyable exercise program for golfers?
- Walking, stair-climbing, cycling, and jogging programs to improve heart and leg fitness
- Muscle strengthening exercises for golfers

WHAT IS A SIMPLE, SAFE, YET BENEFICIAL AND ENJOYABLE EXERCISE PROGRAM FOR GOLFERS?

You know why you should exercise. The benefits are well known and we have gone to some length to discuss them up to this point. But how should you exercise? What is a simple, safe, yet beneficial and enjoyable exercise program for golfers? You have very wisely decided to embark on that journey toward improved health and fitness–with the additional reward of being able to play and enjoy better golf.

So here are some things you should look for in an exercise program regardless of your age, gender, current level of golf, health and fitness, or previous experience with sports or exercise programs:

- *It should be simple.* A good exercise program should be easy to do and ideally, it should be one that can be done at home or in your workplace, and requires little or no special equipment.
- *It should be safe.* Exercise is supposed to help–not hurt or harm. Therefore, your program should be one that can be easily tailored to your needs, particularly your current level of health and fitness.
- *It should be beneficial.* That might seem an obvious statement, but many people who exercise seem to be spinning their wheels. They have the best intentions and even perform some well-meaning exercises. But if the exercises are the wrong ones, done improperly, or for the wrong length of time, these exercises won't do the golfers or their golf much good. And, in some cases, the wrong program could even do some harm to their health or golf.
- *It should be enjoyable.* Being notorious for their aversion to exercise, golfers need an exercise program that hopefully they can gain some

pleasure from. Failing that, the program should at least be one that is not unpleasant because it results in discomfort or is difficult to do regularly as it needs special skills, equipment, space, or environmental conditions.

- *It should be brief.* Most recreational golfers will only agree to an exercise program that takes no more than about 30 minutes to do, is not so strenuous or tiring that they need more than another 30 minutes to recover fully from. The reason is that the majority of golfers who have more than an hour to spare would probably prefer spending that time hitting balls, chipping, and putting, or even playing four or more holes of golf.
- *It should provide immediate feedback.* Golfers want results and they want them *now.* That's why they spend so much money buying equipment and balls that they think will improve their game immediately. They want the same from their exercise program. They want to be able to feel or measure the benefits within a relatively short time.

If you are not very unfit or do not have any significant or serious medical problems, the following is an example of a proper exercise program that will meet the above requirements and the "FITT" formula exercise prescription recommended earlier in Hole No. 4:

- Start with at least three to five minutes of warm-up walking, stretching, or calisthenic exercises.
- Go on to 20 minutes of a fairly continuous aerobic activity of your choice (e.g., walking, stair-climbing, running in place, cycling, dancing, jogging) to improve the fitness of your heart, lungs and leg muscles, as these are the most important for golf.
- End with at least three to five minutes of cool-down walking, stretching, or calisthenic exercises, followed by at least another three to five minutes of rest and relaxation.

All these exercises should be done at an intensity appropriate to your current level of health and fitness. The total time for each exercise session would therefore be less than 30 minutes. Frequency of exercise should be at least three times a week and on fairly well-spaced out days. It should not be only a weekend exercise program. The total minimum time of 90 minutes a week required (30 minutes per session, three times a week) for such an exercise program may appear to many golfers to be too time-consuming. However, one should compare it with other apparently more important activities. Most golfers seem willing to spend five to ten minutes a day (or 35 to 70 minutes per week) to brush and shave (for men) or apply make-up (for ladies) to look and feel good. Then surely, spending 90 minutes a week to look after the physical well-being of your body and mind–and to improve your golf–cannot be considered an unreasonable demand.

If you have significant medical or fitness problems, appropriate modifications to the above recommended program have to be made, bearing in mind that the principles of warm-up, aerobic, and cool-down exercises need to be followed as closely as possible.

WALKING

One attractive feature of walking–along with stair-climbing, running in place, cycling and jogging–is that, unlike most sports and games, these are individual physical activities that can be done at a golfer's own convenience, pace, needs, capabilities, and in accordance with the "FITT" formula exercise prescription outlined in Hole No. 4.

There are three main types of walking: leisurely normal-paced walking, brisk or pace-walking, and competitive race-walking. For the very unfit golfer, leisurely walking at a normal pace and for relatively brief periods of time is a safe and useful activity to help improve aerobic (heart-lung-blood circulation) fitness, and the strength and endurance of your leg muscles, ligaments and joints. For all others, brisk walking or pace-walking is a safe and effective way to improve overall health and fitness, particularly aerobic fitness, and for reduction of excess body fat.

Pace-walking is also a very good activity to help unfit golfers improve their health and fitness before they take up more vigorous activities such as tennis or jogging. Race-walking is normally faster, more strenuous and may be equivalent in intensity to jogging, or even running.

Pace-walking should be tailored to your own needs, capabilities and in accordance with the "FITT" formula exercise prescription recommendations outlined in Hole No. 4, and as follows:

- Level 1: Pace-walk 20 to 30 minutes 3 to 5 times a week, or 10 to 20 minutes 6 to 7 times a week.
- Level 2: Pace-walk 30 to 45 minutes 3 to 5 times a week, or 20 to 30 minutes 6 to 7 times a week.
- Level 3: Pace-walk 45 to 60 minutes 3 to 5 times a week, or 30 to 45 minutes 6 to 7 times a week.

Do not proceed to the next level until you can pace-walk comfortably at your present level. Pace-walk at a speed that is comfortable for you. Most people are able to pace-walk comfortably at speeds of about three miles per hour or 100 paces per minute. When pace-walking, keep your head, shoulders, and body fairly upright without being stiff or uncomfortable. Keep your arms relaxed, slightly bent, and swing them naturally to help you maintain rhythm and balance. *If you want to expend more energy while pace-walking, pump your arms.* Your feet should land gently on your heels and roll smoothly onto your toes.

It is recommended that you pace-walk in a pair of good walking, jogging, running, or other sports shoes. Such shoes need not be expensive, but should be light, flexible, well-padded, and well fitting with proper arch and heel supports. If you decide to pace-walk on the road, observe traffic regulations and personal safety precautions: face oncoming traffic; walk on pavements or footpaths if available; and wear light-colored attire, preferably with luminous reflectors for walking when it is dark.

STAIR-CLIMBING, BENCH-STEPPING OR STEP-UPS

Studies have shown that low-fit, middle-aged, sedentary people who averaged 25 to 30 flights of stairs a day for about five days a week, over a 10 to 12-week period, were able to very significantly improve their cardio-respiratory fitness and decrease their body fat. Such stair-climbing was done at a normal comfortable pace of less than about 100 steps per minute, and was not necessarily done continuously in one session.

For maximum benefits and minimum risks, stair-climbing, bench-stepping or step-ups should be done according to the "FITT" formula exercise prescription outlined in Hole No. 4. The following programs are recommended:

- Level 1: Stair-climb, bench-step or step-up fairly continuously for 3 to 5 minutes, 3 to 5 times a week.
- Level 2: Stair-climb, bench-step or step-up fairly continuously for 5 to 10 minutes, 3 to 5 times a week.
- Level 3: Stair-climb, bench-step or step-up fairly continuously for 10 to 20 minutes 3 to 5 times a week.
- Level 4: Stair-climb, bench-step or step-up fairly continuously for 20 to 30 minutes, 3 to 5 times a week.
- Level 5: Stair-climb, bench-step or step-up fairly continuously for 30 to 60 minutes, 3 to 5 times a week.

Do not proceed to the next level until you can stair-climb, bench-step or step-up comfortably at your present level.

CYCLING

Cycling is not only a good aerobic exercise, it can also be fun. People who ride bicycles for health's sake mostly either ride stationary indoor bicycles, ride for fun, or ride to and from work. Some people who take up this activity with a passion, ride competitively. Cycling, combined with stretching or calisthenic exercises, is particularly recommended for golfers who are overweight and are looking for a physical activity that is not too stressful on the muscles, ligaments, and joints of the lower limbs. This is especially important for those who have medical or orthopedic problems, or injuries involving the weight-bearing joints of the lower limbs, such as the hip, knee and ankle joints.

You don't have to spend a great deal of money on a bicycle that will perform in the ways that you need. Many of today's bicycles are manufactured of light-weight materials that make cycling much easier. And, those bikes with gears perform the same function.

The following program is recommended for both indoor or outdoor cycling:

- Level 1: Cycle fairly continuously for 5 to 10 minutes, 3 to 5 times a week.
- Level 2: Cycle fairly continuously for 10 to 20 minutes, 3 to 5 times a week.
- Level 3: Cycle fairly continuously for 20 to 30 minutes, 3 to 5 times a week.
- Level 4: Cycle fairly continuously for 30 to 60 minutes, 3 to 5 times a week.

Do not proceed to the next level until you can cycle comfortably at your present level. Cycle at a speed or resistance that is comfortable for you. As with other exercise programs, if you cannot pass the "talk-test" (which is your ability to carry on a normal conversation while exercising), you are probably cycling faster or harder than you should. Cycle in a style that is comfortable for you. However, it is recommended that you keep your back and lower limbs fairly upright and relaxed. Pedal on the balls of your feet (not instep or heels) and adjust the seat height so that your knee is nearly straight at the bottom of the downstroke. By doing so, you use more of your quadriceps muscles, which give you more power, allow you to cycle longer, and burn more calories.

Many people favor stationary indoor cycling. Health clubs are full of them. If you live in a climate that is not conducive to cycling or exercising outdoors for much of the year, indoor cycling would be ideal for you. You don't have to contend with the traffic, nor do you need to worry about riding up and down hills or curves. You can easily regulate the amount of exercise you get. If you have heart, lung, or leg problems, this could be the answer for you. Before you consider indoor cycling as too boring, many people ride stationary cycles while listening to music, watching television or reading. Indoor stationary bicycles need not be expensive, but should have a smooth and even pedal resistance that is easily adjustable for different intensities of exercise. For safety and comfort, such bicycles should also be stable and adjustable for seat and handlebar height.

JOGGING

Jogging remains as one of the best ways to get into a high level of health and fitness. It requires no special equipment, outside of a good pair of running shoes. It can be highly beneficial to the heart and lungs, while contributing to good overall fitness. However, as jogging is a more rigorous exercise or physical activity than walking, stair-climbing, or cycling, golfers who are not sufficiently fit are advised to start with a walking exercise program, followed by alternately walking and jogging for at least 4 to 12 weeks before beginning a serious jogging program. Since most golfers are in the less fit group, emphasis in this book will be on the less rigorous activities described earlier, and only some information regarding jogging will be presented. Fitter golfers who are interested in more details regarding jogging are advised to refer to other publications listed at the end of this book that are recommended for further reading, such as my book entitled **"Sports Medicine, Exercise and Fitness: A Guide for Everyone."**

Jogging is non-competitive running, mainly for health and fitness, at speeds below 7 mph or 9 minutes per mile. When combined with stretches or calisthenics (e.g., toe-touching, trunk-twisting and arm-swinging), jogging is ideal for developing and maintaining a high level of overall health and fitness. If done properly, jogging is an enjoyable, convenient, simple, safe and beneficial form of exercise for young and old, male and female.

The following are some tips to help you jog safely, comfortably and effectively:

- Look ahead with your head and body relaxed and fairly upright.
- Breathe naturally through your mouth, nose, or both.
- Your arms should be relaxed and comfortable (e.g., low arm-swing action with lightly-held fists).
- Wear loose, lightweight, porous, short-sleeved T-shirt, and shorts when the weather is warm, and adequate protective attire against the cold and wind when the weather is cold and the wind chill factor is significant.
- You should wear light-weight, flexible, well-padded, well-fitting jogging, running, or other good sports shoes, that have good heel and arch supports. If your shoe is well-padded and has good insole support, you may not need to wear socks or have insole supports, unless you are very overweight, or have foot or heel problems.
- While jogging, your knees should be slightly bent at all times and you should have a heel-to-toe landing action–unlike sprinting where you run mainly on the front of your feet.
- You should have a comfortable stride. If you feel any discomfort, you should understride rather than overstride.
- Jog or walk-jog according to your own needs, capabilities and in accordance with the "FITT" formula exercise prescription recommendations outlined in Hole No. 4.

The following jog or walk-jog program is recommended:

- Level 1: Walk briskly 20 to 30 minutes 3 to 5 times a week.
- Level 2: Walk briskly 30 to 60 minutes 3 to 5 times a week.
- Level 3: Walk-jog 20 to 30 minutes 3 to 5 times a week.
- Level 4: Jog 20 to 30 minutes 3 to 5 times a week.
- Level 5: Jog 30 to 60 minutes 3 to 5 times a week.

Do not proceed to the next level until you can walk-jog or jog comfortably at your present level. Always jog at a speed which is comfortable for you, and use the "talk-test" or heart rate as a guide to the correct speed or intensity. If you are at level 4 or 5, you are probably exercising at a level in which you should consider its effect on free radical release and take the appropriate actions to consume sufficient antioxidants as outlined in Hole No. 2. For even more details, please refer to more recent publications on free radicals and antioxidants such as ***Dr. Kenneth H. Cooper's The Antioxidant Revolution.***

Should a cramp develop, rest and slowly stretch the muscle, while taking slow and deep breaths. However, it must be remembered that for calf muscle cramps, dorsiflexing the ankle (pushing the foot upward) more than 90^0 may cause more pain, discomfort and further injury. A stitch is a discomfort that develops on one side of the abdomen or the lower chest with the jolting action of jogging. Stitches may be prevented by adequate training, particularly strengthening of abdominal muscles. Stitches may be relieved by slow and deep breathing, change of posture (such as bending forward and sideway), and hand-pressure over the site of pain.

MUSCLE STRENGTHENING EXERCISES FOR GOLFERS

Unlike weightlifting, football, and other more rigorous sports, golf is not a game that depends as much on strength for successful performance. However, golf still does require strength to some extent to hit the ball further without loss of accuracy and to prevent injuries–which is particularly important for the majority of recreational golfers who have below desirable levels of muscle strength. Therefore, you should include at least a minimal muscle strengthening exercise program as part of your overall improvement program for your health, fitness, and golf.

The two main types of exercises to improve strength are calisthenics and those using free weights or resistance machines. Like most non-golfers, the majority of golfers prefer to exercise on their time at home or at the workplace, hopefully without having to invest in any special equipment or machines–whether they be simple, inexpensive free weights like dumb-bells, or the more complicated and expensive resistance machines touted on television, in newspapers and magazines.

Therefore, most of the exercises recommended for you in this book would be calisthenic exercises. These exercises can easily be done at your home or workplace with no need for any special equipment except the one you carry with you all the time–your body. This is because calisthenic exercises use mainly your own body weight and the force of gravity to help increase your muscle strength. Examples of these exercises are push-ups, pull-ups, sit-ups, "crunches", back-raisers, step-ups, and calf-raisers.

The additional advantage of calisthenic exercises is that you can also do them conveniently when you are traveling–as many golfers do for business or pleasure–and staying in a room without much space, or a facility that has no gym or equipment. Before describing the recommended calisthenic exercises, it is important to be clear about how they should be safely and correctly done, and the terms to be used.

- A "repetition" is defined as one complete movement of the exercise and a "set" is a group of repetitions done continuously.
- After each set of exercise, you should rest for about 20 to 30 seconds before proceeding to the next set or type of calisthenic exercise.
- You should not hold your breath while doing any exercises. Breathe in before starting and breathe out while doing each repetition.
- The number of repetitions you should do for each calisthenic exercise depends on the muscles to be strengthened–usually more repetitions for the stronger lower limb muscles and fewer for the weaker upper limb muscles.
- The type of calisthenic exercise also determines the number of repetitions–fewer repetitions for pull-ups because your upper limb muscles have to carry your whole body weight while more repetitions in push-ups as they have to work against less weight.
- Your current level of your strength, health, and fitness also influence the number of repetitions and the way you should do the exercise. For example, you should do fewer repetitions if you are not fit now–and more when you become fitter.
- As the strength of your muscles increases, you should modify the exercise to increase the workload resistance for those muscles, otherwise you will not be able to continue to increase the strength of the muscles involved.
- If you are not strong enough to do a particular exercise now (e.g., regular push-up), start with modified ones (e.g., push-ups from the knees).
- For all calisthenic exercises, except the whole-body weight exercise for upper limb muscles like the pull-up, you should generally aim to eventually be able to complete three sets of 8 to 12 repetitions without developing muscle soreness, pain, discomfort, or other medical problems (e.g., giddiness, breathlessness, chest pains).
- Initially, if you are unfit, you should start with fewer repetitions per set. When you can easily complete three sets of 12 repetitions, you should make the exercise more difficult by increasing the number of repetitions in each set, or add a fourth or fifth set of exercises.
- For a comprehensive muscle strength training program for golf, you should do calisthenic exercises for the major muscles of the upper limbs (e.g., push-ups), abdomen (e.g., sit-ups), back (e.g., back-raisers), and lower limbs (e.g., step-ups).
- You can do these exercises for the different muscle groups separately.

- You can also do them in a circuit, for example, start by doing one set of 8 push-ups, then one set of 8 sit-ups, one set of 8 back-raisers, and end with one set of 12 step-ups. Rest for 20 to 30 seconds, and repeat this circuit two to three times.
- Calisthenic exercises should be done at least two to three times a week on evenly spaced out days.
- They should take 20 to 30 minutes for each exercise session.

Regular Push-Ups

Rest your weight on palms of your hand and your toes. Your palms should be about shoulder-width apart, and your back, arms, and elbows straight. Using only your arms, lower your body to the surface without actually touching it. Then push your body up so that your elbows are straight again.

This complete movement constitutes one repetition. Aim to do two or more sets of 8 to 12 repetitions.

Modified Bent-Knee Push-Ups

If you are not yet strong enough to do regular push-ups, start with bent-knee push-ups that are identical with regular push-ups except that you rest your weight on your palms and knees (instead of toes).

Bent-Knee Sit-Ups

Lie flat on your back with your arms in front of you and your knees bent about 90° and feet flat on the surface. Raise your upper body to a near sitting position, then lower your body back to the surface.

This complete movement constitutes one repetition. Aim to do two or more sets of 8 to 12 repetitions. If you are not yet strong enough to do a full sit-up, do a half or quarter sit-up where you bring your upper body part of the way up instead.

Back-Raisers

Lie flat on your front with your hands on your buttocks. Slowly lift your head, chest, and both legs together about 6 to 12 inches off the surface while keeping your knees fairly straight. Return to the start position. This complete movement constitutes one repetition. Aim to do two or more sets of 8 to 12 repetitions.

Modified Back-Raisers

If you are not yet strong enough to do a full back-raiser, do a simpler one by raising only your head and chest first–supported on your elbows –then both your legs together or separately.

Step-Ups

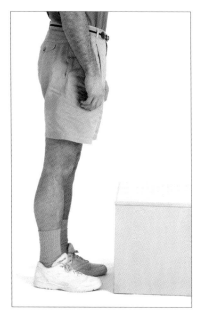

For this exercise, you need a strong and stable step, stool, chair, stairs, or ladder, preferably about the height of your knees.

Keeping your body fairly straight, step up with one leg until your knee is straight at the top of the step before stepping down. This complete movement constitutes one repetition.

Aim to do two or more sets of 12 or more repetitions for each leg in turn.

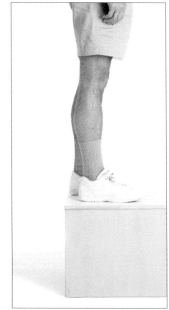

You should try to do the golf-fitness exercises outlined in this chapter as often and as regularly as you can. Like everything else in life, if you plan ahead of time and put these exercises into your daily life, just as you do any other important matter (e.g., a business meeting or appointment), you are more likely to find the time and remember to do them.

It is not essential that you do all the exercises outlined or in the sequence presented. Choose the exercises which are most suitable for your needs and which you enjoy most. To overcome the boredom of doing the same exercise every day or week, you should consider changing them on a weekly, fortnightly, or monthly basis.

As an example, you may wish to walk in the first fortnight, cycle in the next and stair-climb the next month. Besides making your exercise program less boring, such cross-training is beneficial to your body. This is because all these aerobic exercises have slightly different demands and emphasis of the different muscles in your body.

Doing the exercises in the sequence outlined in this chapter has the advantage that you are less likely to forget to do an exercise to strengthen that part of your body.

Hole No. 8

EXERCISES YOU CAN DO TO PREVENT OR TREAT COMMON GOLF INJURIES

- Lower back problems
- "Golfer's elbow" and other upper limb injuries
- Knee and other lower limb injuries

LOWER BACK PROBLEMS

About 80% of people would experience lower back pain and problems to varying degrees of severity some time in their life. If you have suffered a "slipped disc" or other serious problems as I did, you would know how painful and debilitating it can be. Therefore, it is essential that you take care of your back and prevent lower back problems by remembering and doing a few simple precautionary measures. This is particularly important for golfers because a bad back will, among other things, keep you off the golf course for an extended period of time–and no true golfer wants that!

As mentioned in previous chapters, I suffered a severe "slipped" disc in the lower back–with sciatica–after carrying a golf bag and suitcase which were too heavy for me during a golf trip five years ago. After deciding against surgery as the first treatment option, I treated myself with judicious rest, medication, very intensive stretching and strengthening back exercises. Within three months, I recovered sufficiently to resume playing competitive golf. Since then, I have been even more conscious of the need to avoid activities that may cause or aggravate lower back problems. I also continue to do the recommended exercises daily to strengthen and stretch the muscles and ligaments of the lower back.

From my professional and personal experiences, and those of my fellow golfers and patients with bad lower back problems, it is particularly beneficial that these exercises (like many others) be done when you wake up in the morning before you start any physical activities–perhaps even before getting out of bed! The reason is that your back, like many other parts of your body, is often tightest and stiffest in the morning because of the relatively poor blood circulation. This is due to a combination of factors such as the relatively low room temperature in the morning, and the hours of low blood circulation due to sleep and inactivity.

Back exercises, when done properly, would help to significantly improve blood flow, warm up your back muscles, increase its flexibility, reduce muscle spasm and pain. You should therefore do your back exercises just before, during, and immediately after a round of golf or other physical activities (e.g., gardening).

It is not advisable to bend your back forward in a standing position with your knees straight. This is because studies have shown that this puts excessive stress and strain on the muscles, ligaments, and joints in your lumbar-sacral spine and may cause or aggravate lower back problems, including "slipped" discs. If you must bend your back forward in the standing position, then you should keep your knees slightly bent, preferably with one foot in front of the other.

At the Golf Course

- Use a light golf bag. They are easier to carry and are better for the back.
- A dual-strap arrangement is also easier on the back. The bag's weight is distributed more evenly and the pressure is not on one side of the body.
- Don't overload your golf bag. Remove excess baggage and take only what you will need for that day's round of golf.
- If you have to carry more, put some of the load (e.g., extra golf balls, sweater, rain suit) in a separate tote bag. Two lighter bags are easier on the back than one heavy overloaded bag.
- If you have a back problem or are not in very good physical condition, use the bag drop if the course has one available. The attendant will carry your bag to the cart staging area–that enables you to park farther from the clubhouse. That gives you the extra benefit of a brisk warm-up aerobic walk from the parking lot.
- When lifting a heavy golf bag, suitcase, or other loads, always try to keep your back fairly straight, stand as close to the load as possible, and bend your knees and hips. ***Then lift mainly with your leg muscles which– in most golfers– are usually at least two to four times stronger than their back or arm muscles.***
- If you have to walk and carry a heavy golf bag or other loads for several minutes, stop and rest after every 30 to 60 seconds. Do not wait until you feel any pain or discomfort.
- When you resume, alternately carry the bag over the other shoulder.

If you are using a motorized golf cart, do not sit in a slouching position as that is not good for your back, especially if you already have an existing back problem.

Try to sit as upright as possible, with your back fairly straight but relaxed.

At The Tee-Box and Putting Green

Do the warm-up aerobic and stretching exercises for your back (as outlined in Hole No. 5) before you hit the first ball on the practice range or first tee. The final warm-up exercise for the back and the rest of the body just before you hit your first ball should be to slowly make a golf swing (with your golf club) but only at about 50% of your normal swing intensity. Do this exercise for about 30 to 60 seconds, then rest for 15 to 30 seconds. Repeat this final warm-up exercise, gradually increasing the speed and intensity of your swing by 10% every minute until you reach about 90% of your normal swing. This procedure should only take you five minutes, and will go a long way to improving your golf shots for the day and in preventing (or aggravating) back or other injuries.

It is not advisable to bend forward with your knees straight when teeing the ball or retrieving it from the hole.

Ideally, you should keep your back as straight as possible, then bend both knees until you get into a near full or full squatting position. One possible reason why women golfers have fewer lower back problems is because they are more likely to adopt this ideal position than men golfers. If, like many golfers, you have tight calf muscles and Achilles tendons, and have difficulty squatting, then do what is recommended on the next page.

*The best alternative to squatting–which many golfers have diffi-
culty doing because of their tight calf muscles and Achilles tendons–is
to bend your front knee slightly, then taking some load off your lower
back by holding on to a golf club with your free hand and leaning
on it to put some of your body weight on the club. This is regardless of
whether you are teeing the ball or retrieving it from the hole.*

Home And Workplace

Adjust the height of your chairs, tables, and other furniture in your home and workplace so that they are at the correct height. This varies from person to person (depending mainly on his or her height) and is that which allows you to work efficiently. If you have to bend forward at the waist more than about 30° for more than a few minutes at a time, that table is too low for you and your back.

If you cannot raise this table higher and have to bend forward at the waist for more than a few seconds, get some telephone books to raise the item and support as much of your weight as possible on your hands by placing your hand or hands on the table and leaning on them. Also place one of your feet about 6 to 12 inches in front of the other, then relax and bend both your hips and knees slightly to reduce the stress on your lower back.

The Sitting Position

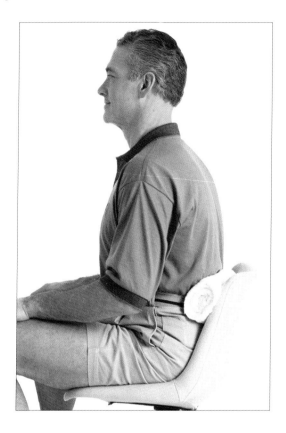

Sit as upright as you comfortably can with as much support for your lower back as possible. If your chair or seat in your home, workplace, or car does not have a good lumbar support, you don't have to buy a special lumbar support device if you don't wish to.

The easiest thing to do is to *place a rolled-up towel or small pillow between the small of your back and the back of the chair or seat*, and often it will work just as well–and sometimes even better. Try to keep your knees at the same level or only slightly higher than your hips, but never so high that your hips and knees are bent more than 90°

When driving, try to keep your legs fairly straight. Your hips and knees should not be bent more than 90°. When making the bed or doing other chores at low heights, you should bend your knees or even kneel, rather than stoop over and bend too much at the waist.

Other **"do's"** for the back include:

- Do exercise regularly but correctly (especially exercises for the back).
- Do adopt a good and correct posture when sitting or standing (as straight as possible, keeping head high, looking forward, and abdomen pulled in).
- Do sleep on a firm (not hard) mattress or surface, and sleeping on your back, side or front (but preferably not semi-prone).
- Do wear well-fitting shoes and avoiding those with high heels.
- Do "walk through" your golf shot like many senior professional golfers now do.

Other **"don'ts"** for the back include:

- Don't go into the "reverse C" position during the follow-through after swinging a golf club.
- Don't lift heavy golf bags or other objects alone; ask for help from stronger persons and those without back problems.
- Don't perform sudden movements of the back, especially forward-bending combined with rapid twisting to the side.
- Don't overstretch or over-tire the back muscles and ligaments.
- Don't put on extra weight that will force your lumbar spine to curve more forward (hyperlordosis) causing more stress to the lower back.
- Don't allow your anterior abdominal ("stomach") muscles to be loose and sag as this would have a similar effect on the lower back to having a paunch or "beer belly."

Back Exercises

Your back muscles can give you all the support you need if you strengthen them through regular and correct exercises. All exercises should be done within pain-free limits and on a firm (not hard) and even surface. Examples of a good surface would be a carpeted floor or a bed with a firm mattress.

If there is discomfort, fatigue or pain, reduce the intensity of the exercise or the number of repetitions. If the symptoms still persist, stop doing that exercise. If your back muscles are tight, relax and take a warm shower or warm bath before starting the back exercises. When you first do these exercises, you may feel a mild ache. This should disappear in a few days as your muscles become stronger.

Aim to do 10 to 15 repetitions per exercise eventually. However, at the beginning of any new exercise program, you should do only the number of repetitions you comfortably can and within your pain-free limits. Start with one set of exercises and gradually increase eventually to three to five sets as you improve. Do your exercises daily or minimally three times a week on non-consecutive days.

The best time to exercise is any time that is convenient for you to exercise regularly and without too many interruptions or distractions. However, avoid exercising within two hours of a heavy meal. Many golfers with lower back problems find that doing most of their back exercises first thing in the morning **before** they get out of bed has the added advantage of warming up and loosening the back muscles.

Before starting on any of the recommended back exercises, you should warm up and loosen the back muscles and ligaments by lying flat on your back with your hips and knees bent about 90º, and feet flat on the surface. Then for at least three to five minutes, sway your knees from side to side, and alternately bringing one knee at a time toward your body (without having to actually touch the body) as if you are cycling in a horizontal position.

Lower Back Stretches For Flexibility

Relax and lie flat on your back with arms by your sides, knees bent about 90° and feet flat on surface. Wrap both arms behind your thighs near your knees and slowly pull both knees toward your chest as far as you comfortably can. Feel the stretch in your lower back (but no pain) and hold for 10 to 15 seconds while breathing normally.

Back Rotations

Relax and lie flat on your back with arms by your sides and knees bent less than 45°. Keeping left knee slightly bent, bring right knee to vertical position. Hold outside of right knee with left hand and slowly pull right knee toward left hip while keeping back as flat on surface as possible. Feel stretch (but no pain) on right side of body and back. Hold for 10 to 15 seconds while breathing normally. Return to start position and relax for 15 to 30 seconds before repeating exercise with left knee. Do these two rotation exercises and the back stretching exercise in turn 3 to 5 times.

Half Sit-Ups

Relax and lie flat on your back, with arms by side, knees bent about 90° and feet flat on surface. Raise hands to top of knees and slowly raise head and chest to a half sit-up position as much as you comfortably can. Feel anterior abdominal ("stomach") muscles contract and back stretch (but no pain). Hold position for 10 to 15 seconds while breathing normally. Slowly return to the start position and relax for 15 to 30 seconds before repeating this exercise 3 to 5 times.

Back Strengtheners

Relax and lie flat on your back, with arms by side, knees bent about 90° and feet flat on surface. Slowly press small of back against surface by tightening back, buttock and "stomach" muscles. Hold position for 10 to 15 seconds while breathing normally. Relax for 15 to 30 seconds before repeating exercise 3 to 5 times.

Back Extensors

Relax, lie on your front and on your forearms and elbows. Slowly lift your head and chest as high up as you comfortably can while keeping your forearms and elbows on the surface. Feel the contraction and stretch of your back muscles and spine (but no pain). Hold position for 10 to 15 seconds while breathing normally. Slowly return to the start position and relax for 15 to 30 seconds before repeating this exercise 3 to 5 times.

Back Raisers or Hyperextension Exercise

When you are fit enough, slowly lift your head, chest and both legs together about 6 to 12 inches off the surface while keeping your knees fairly straight. You should feel a strain (but no pain) in your back muscles. Hold position for 10 to 15 seconds while breathing normally. Slowly return to the start position and relax for 15 to 30 seconds before repeating this exercise 3 to 5 times.

"GOLFER'S ELBOW" AND OTHER UPPER LIMB INJURIES

"Golfer's Elbow" and "Tennis Elbow"

These injuries can cause anything from a mild discomfort to a severe pain around the elbow. They are partial tear injuries to the tendons of your forearm muscles where they originate from the elbow. "Golfer's elbow", or medial epicondylitis, is the injury to the tendons of the wrist and finger flexor muscles which originate on the medial or inner side of your elbow. "Tennis Elbow" or lateral epicondylitis, is the injury to the tendons of the wrist and finger extensor muscles which originate on the lateral or outer side of your elbow.

Both these injuries are fairly common among golfers and others who put stress on the muscles of their arms and wrists (e.g., tennis players, manual workers). Nearly all golfers experience these injuries to varying degrees at least a few times in their golf lifetime.

However, golfers who are most likely to get frequent recurrences of these injuries are those:

- With forearm and wrist muscles that are weak or are not strong enough for the excessive stress put on them (e.g., using a heavy golf club, over-swinging).
- Older golfers, especially those over 40 years of age.
- Who do not warm up their forearm muscles adequately or correctly (as outlined in Hole No. 5).
- Who try to hit the ball too hard, or use too much of their forearm and wrist muscles.
- Who take large divots or hit hard objects (e.g., stones, rocks, tree roots, firm sand in sandtraps or bunkers, hard rubber mats at practice ranges).
- With incorrect golf swing, grip, or club.

Both these injuries often take some time to heal completely–usually at least three to six weeks–and are difficult to treat because of:

- The poor blood supply of the injured tissues–that is why tendons are whitish in color compared with the reddish muscle bellies.
- The golfer is usually in the older age group–older persons take longer to recover from the same injuries compared with younger persons.

> ■ The long delay before proper treatment is sought or given.
> ■ The difficulty in resting the injured tendons sufficiently enough to allow the injury to heal properly, despite the golfer slowing down the swing, not hitting so hard or even stopping golf. This is because the muscles of these tendons are used frequently and extensively in our daily lives and the injured tendons continue to be stressed.

The way to prevent these injuries is through gradual and proper warm-up and exercise. The muscles surrounding the tendons must be properly stretched and strengthened to prevent damage to the tendons. In the meantime, wearing a forearm brace–you've seen PGA Tour players wear them from time to time–will keep some of the pressure off the tendons, thus alleviating some of the pain. In the extreme case, the elbow may have to be put in a sling or a cast. Some injuries may require an injection of cortisone or other steroids, or may become so serious that surgery may be required. Thankfully, that is generally not the case. Most of such injuries can be treated (as outlined in Hole No. 6) with the "RICE" method, anti-inflammatory medication, physical therapy, exercises, and changes in the golf swing or style of play.

Exercises for "Golfer's Elbow"

Note: "Tennis elbow" is similar to "golfer's elbow" except that it is an injury to the tendon of the antagonistic or opposing muscle. Therefore, when stretching and increasing the flexibility of the muscle for "golfer's elbow", you would be contracting and strengthening the muscle of the tendon for "tennis elbow", and vice versa.

Since the exercises to prevent or treat both injuries are similar, the exercises outlined below for "golfer's elbow" are also for "tennis elbow", except in the reverse direction.

Stretching Exercises

Please refer to Hole No. 5 where these exercises have been described.

Forearm, Wrist, And Finger Extensor Muscle Strengthening Exercise

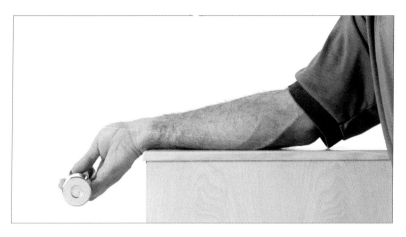

You need a dumb-bell, book, or any other object which you can comfortably hold in one hand. The weight of the object you choose should depend on the state of your present strength or injury. Place your forearm on a support (e.g., edge of a table) with your palm facing up and wrist over the edge. Hold the book (or other object) in your hand and bend your wrist upward. Hold position for 10 to 15 seconds while breathing normally and feeling the strain (but no pain) in your forearm muscles. Relax for 15 to 30 seconds, then repeat this exercise 10 to 15 times for each hand. Increase the weight as you get stronger but always exercise within pain-free limits.

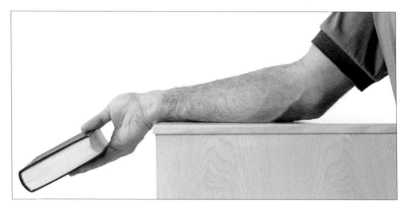

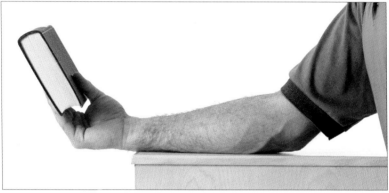

All of these exercises for the prevention or treatment of "golfer's elbow" can be used for "tennis elbow" except that you do them in the reverse direction. For example, the book should be held over the table edge with the palm facing down as in the photo below.

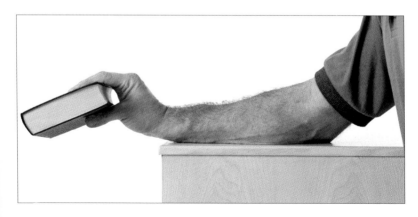

Additional Strengthening Exercise For "Tennis Elbow"

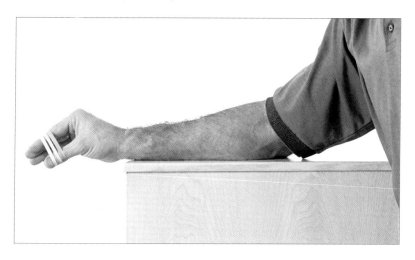

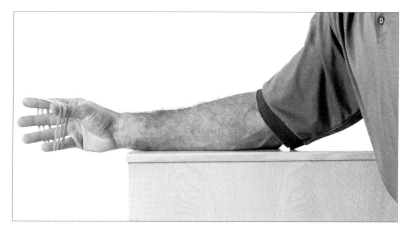

You need rubber bands. Close your thumb and fingers together and point them away from you. Choose 3 to 10 rubber bands (the actual number depends on the type of band, your present strength or injury) and place them over your fingers. Keeping the elbow fairly straight, stretch the rubber bands by opening your thumb and fingers.

Hold position for 10 to 15 seconds while breathing normally and feeling the strain (but no pain) in your forearm muscles. Relax for 15 to 30 seconds, then repeat this exercise 10 to 15 times for each hand. Increase the number of rubber bands as you get stronger but always exercise within pain-free limits.

Forearm, Wrist, and Grip Strengthening Exercise

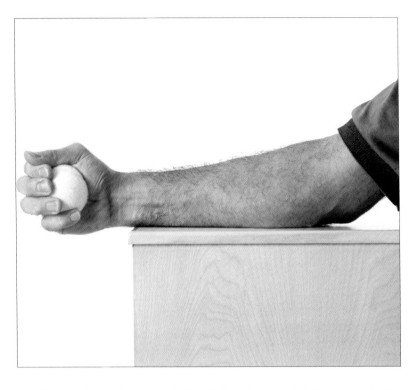

You need a golf or tennis ball, rolled-up handkerchief, or other similar objects you can grip comfortably (e.g., steering wheel while you are driving).

Keeping the elbow fairly straight, grip the object as hard as you comfortably can but within pain-free limits, and hold position for 10 to 15 seconds while breathing normally.

Relax for 15 to 30 seconds, then repeat this exercise 10 to 15 times for each hand.

Shoulder Problems

Most "frozen" or painful shoulders in golfers are due more to chronic overuse injuries than acute injuries. Many are due to recurrent minor tears of the rotator cuff muscles or the long head of the biceps muscles that result in excessive fibrous or scar tissue formation and eventually stiffness of the shoulder. They are more common among older golfers and those with a past history or excessive stress on the shoulder or recurrent shoulder injuries.

Prevention of such conditions in golfers includes proper warm-up and stretching exercises (see Hole No. 5), gradual increase in stress or training loads, avoiding overuse, and stopping the cause at the earliest sign of injury (i.e., pain in the shoulder). Treatment consists of "RICE" treatment and other therapy outlined in Hole No. 6, stretching and strengthening exercises as outlined below. In addition to the stretching exercise outlined in Hole No. 5, the following two exercises can be done at home or in the workplace.

"Doorway" Stretches

Relax and stand upright with your feet about shoulder-width apart in an open doorway with the open door in front of you (or between 2 vertical bars or other structures of similar width as a doorway). Lift both arms sideways up to the height of your head and hold onto the door-frames on both sides of the doorway. Take a small step forward and slowly lean forward as far as you comfortably can until you feel stretch (but no pain) over the front of both shoulders and chest. Hold position for 10 to 15 seconds while breathing normally. Relax for 15 to 30 seconds, then repeat this exercise 10 to 15 times. Increase the height that you can hold on the door-frames as you get more flexible but always stretch within pain-free limits.

(*Note:* Although it is easier and faster to do this exercise with both hands and shoulders, it can also be done with one arm and shoulder at a time if you prefer to do so for whatever reason.)

"Walk"-Up-The-Wall Stretches

Stand relaxed and fairly upright with your feet about shoulder-width apart and your left side nearly an arm's length from a wall, door or other vertical structure. Bring your left hand up and horizontally until your fingers just touch the wall. Without moving your body, slowly let your fingers "walk" up the wall as high as you comfortably can until you feel stretch (but no pain) in your shoulder.

Hold position for 10 to 15 seconds while breathing normally. Relax for 15 to 30 seconds, then repeat this exercise 10 to 15 times for each shoulder. Increase the height you can "walk" up the wall as you get more flexible but always stretch within pain-free limits.

KNEE AND OTHER LOWER LIMB INJURIES

Injuries to the muscles, tendons and ligaments in and around the knee, ankle, and foot joint complexes are common in sports like golf which require some twisting action in the lower limbs.

Prevention of such injuries include:

- Adequate and proper warm-up and stretching exercises as outlined in Hole No. 5.
- Strengthening exercises (outlined below) and playing within your current level of fitness.
- Correct technique in the golf swing.

First aid treatment of such injuries consist mainly of the "RICE" treatment (outlined in Hole No. 6). Subsequent non-surgical treatment consists of anti-inflammatory medication, physical therapy, and exercises (outlined below).

Knee Injuries

These include partial tears to the medial and lateral collateral ligaments, medial meniscus and lateral meniscus, anterior and posterior cruciate ligaments, and "runner's knee" (also known by some as patello-femoral pain, anterior knee pain, or chondromalacia patella).

In "runner's knee", there is roughening of the posterior surface of the patella (knee cap) as a result of excessive friction between the patella and the lower end of the femur bone (the femoral condyle). This results in pain, discomfort, or instability in the knee especially when walking up or down slopes on the golf course, steps or stairs.

Rehabilitation consists of intensive quadriceps strengthening exercises, especially the last 15° to 30° of extension. However, for many, there may be pain or discomfort when doing leg extension exercises from 90° flexion to full extension. If so, such exercises should only be done in the pain-free range (e.g., from 15° to 30° flexion to full extension).

Specific static quadriceps exercises for "runner's knee" can also be done by golfers at home or in the workplace. One such exercise is the "quarter-squat" in which the golfer stands with feet about shoulder-width apart, and bends at the knees by about 30° to 45°, then holds that position (without pain or discomfort) for about 15 minutes, once or twice daily.

Knee Strengtheners

Quadriceps and Calf Muscle Strengthening Exercise

Sit comfortably on a chair, sofa, or bed with both knees straight and toes pointed away from you. Slowly contract your quadriceps and calf muscles as much as you comfortably can until you feel a strain (but no pain or cramps).

Hold position for 10 to 15 seconds while breathing normally. Relax for 15 to 30 seconds, then repeat exercise 10 to 15 times.

Hamstring Strengtheners

Stand comfortably with back to table or wall, and heels about three inches away.

Lift right foot slightly off floor and bend your right knee slightly and slowly push right heel back as hard as you comfortably can until you feel a strain (but no pain) in your hamstring muscles.

Hold position for 10 to 15 seconds while breathing normally.

Calf Muscle And Ankle Strengtheners

Stand comfortably with feet about shoulder-width apart, then tip-toe as high as you comfortably can until you feel a strain (but no pain) in calf muscles.

Balance by holding onto a wall, door, table or chair. Hold position for 10 to 15 seconds while breathing normally.

Then relax for 15 to 30 seconds and repeat this exercise 10 to 15 times.

Plantar Fasciitis, Foot, And Heel Problems

Plantar fasciitis is inflammation of the fibrous plantar fascia (or aponeurosis) which helps maintain the longitudinal arch of the foot. It usually presents as pain, or discomfort on or in front of the heel, and is not uncommon among golfers, especially those who are overweight or in poor physical condition.

Plantar fasciitis may be due to a contusion injury and may be associated with a heel spur, that is an excessive growth of bone where the plantar fascia inserts into the heel bone.

Prevention consists of fat-weight reduction, proper padding, and arch support in the shoes (especially golf shoes because during an 18-hole round of golf, you may walk three to four miles), and foot-muscle strengthening exercises such as the following:

Toe Curls

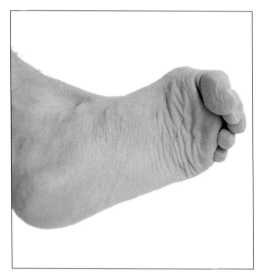

Sit with your feet resting on the floor, then curl downward and back-ward all the toes of both feet as much as you comfortably can until you feel a strain (but no pain) in your foot muscles, ligaments and joints.

Hold position for 10 to 15 seconds while breathing normally.

Then relax for 15 to 30 seconds and repeat this exercise 10 to 15 times.

Toe Spreaders

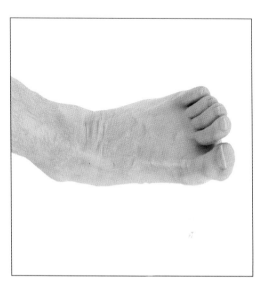

Sit and spread toes in an upward and outward direction as much as you comfortably can until you feel a strain (but no pain) in foot muscles, ligaments and joints.

Hold position for 10 to 15 seconds while breathing normally.

Then relax for 15 to 30 seconds and repeat this exercise 10 to 15 times.

To prevent or reduce the risk of developing common golf injuries, you should try to do all the exercises outlined in this chapter regularly and in accordance with the instructions given for each exercise. These exercises need not be done in the sequence presented although by doing so, you are less likely to neglect or forget any part of your body that is involved in golf.

If you cannot find the time to do all these exercises, you should do as many as you can. Choose those that strengthen the parts of your body which are weaker (e.g., the non-dominant side of your body, especially the muscles and ligaments of the wrist, forearm, and elbow).

While you should do more exercises to strengthen the weaker parts of your body, you should not totally neglect the stronger dominant side. The same principle applies if you have a weaker part of the body due to an injury and which prevents you from playing golf to the best of your ability.

Such a strengthening program will help to correct the strength imbalance between different parts of your body due to different usage or injury. By doing so, you will develop a better golf swing, hit the ball longer and with greater accuracy, and lower your golf scores.

HOLE NO. 9

USING YOUR MIND TO LOWER YOUR GOLF SCORES

- Golf can't be that difficult
- The harder you try, the worse you play
- The "4Cs+1K" prescription to better scores
- Some activities to improve your golf mental fitness

GOLF CAN'T BE THAT DIFFICULT

As mentioned in the Introduction to this book, when I first started playing golf, I thought the game couldn't possibly be difficult. Soon after I started playing golf seriously, I realized that this game is nowhere near as easy as it looks. I also observed that many golfers unwittingly make it even more difficult. Most golfers are prepared to spend countless hours at the practice range to try to improve their swing or lengthen their drives, or at the practice green to groove in their chips and putts.

But, the majority of high handicappers and recreational golfers do not realize the vital contribution their physical and mental health and fitness can make to their game and score. Often these are the areas they neglect most and that is unfortunate because they are areas–especially the mental side–that such golfers can easily improve on in a relatively short period of time when compared with the months it usually takes to adopt and adapt to a new swing.

I am extremely fortunate to have learned my sports psychology formally from Brent S. Rushall, Ph.D., in 1984 while I was doing a major in sports psychology under his supervision. Dr. Rushall is one of the most respected sports psychologists in the world, and is currently a professor specializing in sports psychology at the Department of Physical Education, San Diego State University, California, U.S.A.. He has published 26 books and over 230 articles, book chapters, and psychology tests. They include his 1992 book *"Mental Skills Training For Sports."* This book is one of the recommended references and publications for further reading listed at the end of this book and you should refer to it for further details.

Dr. Rushall has vast knowledge and experience in assisting all types and levels of athletes (including World and Olympic Games athletes) in many sports (including golf). He is therefore very familiar with the psychological problems of amateur, recreational, and professional golfers–and how to overcome them. The information in this chapter comes from what Dr. Rushall has shared with me and from other sports psychologists. However, much of it also comes from my own observations and learning from the better professional and amateur golfers, and my 20 years of personal experiences as a serious and competitive golfer.

From all these information and experiences, I have learned that the following are very true for most golfers, especially the high handicapper, recreational, or occasional golfer:

- *"It's not how you drive but how you arrive"* or as golfers who bet or play for money say *"You drive for show and putt for dough."*
- Although a putt and a drive have equal value of one stroke to your score, with some mental training (e.g., mental imagery), it is usually easier to repeatedly sink a 5- to 10-foot putt than to hit a 250-yard drive down the center of the fairway consistently.
- To lower your golf score more effectively and quickly, you should spend equal or more time practicing your short game on or around the practice green, home, or workplace, as you do for your long game at the practice range.
- The important short game shots to practice are putts of less than 10 feet and chips of less than 30 feet. After all, if for just six holes (or one third of every 18-hole round you play) you can consistently chip to within 5 to 10 feet of the hole and sink half of these putts, you would have saved and lowered your score by three strokes.
- *Learning to chip and putt consistently and successfully is usually more mental than physical.* Therefore they are often more easily learned and consistently reproducible than full physical and more skill-dependent shots such as the drive and fairway shots.
- *"A low score after a round of golf often depends more on how few bad shots you made rather than on how many good ones you produced."* A good 250-yard drive or a 20-foot putt is immediately cancelled by a duff, top, slice, or a hook shot into the rough, or a penalty shot after an OB or going into a hazard.
- Knowing the rules of golf well is a great advantage because you know what your best options are in different situations. That can help you save strokes and mental anguish as you do not penalize yourself more than once.
- An example is dropping your ball within 2 club lengths of where it last crossed the margin of a lateral water hazard and into an

unfavorable lie, when the rules allow other options.
■ Since all the rules of golf can be difficult to recall instantly, especially when you are angry after hitting a bad shot, you need only remember the principles and the more frequently-encountered ones. For the other rules, carry a copy of the rules in your golf bag–as I usually do –for instant reference if and when required.

THE HARDER YOU TRY, THE WORSE YOU PLAY

"The harder you try, the worse you play" applies to golf more often than any other game I know. Golf requires a reasonable amount of skill– but many experts agree it is not a sport that has its success determined mainly by one's athletic ability. Football players can use adrenaline and strength to dominate an opponent. Tennis players can rely on their quickness–and if they try harder, their results are usually better.

Golf, on the other hand, is often just the opposite. Trying harder may simply clutter up the mind and distort the movement pattern of the skill to be used in the shot. Trying harder can also increase the tension in some muscles of the golf swing. That "unbalances" the action and often causes the swing to worsen. On many holes, a clear and calm head can mean the difference between a par or a double bogey.

Your chief opponent is usually not your fellow competitor. It's you (often more your mind than body), the course, and the environmental conditions. The wind could be blowing; it could be raining; greens could be treacherously fast or agonizingly slow; the course could be tight and you might not be the straightest hitter. These are only a few of the many distractions and reasons for adjustments to be made to your golf swing. Some of the alterations increase the uncertainty about your ability to perform the swing and interfere with your skilled movements. This is a common problem in golf. Any number of outside factors could cause your mind to go from positive to negative in a very short time.

Course conditions aside, you also must battle your golf swing. You may have worked hard on your technique or taking many golf lessons at expensive classes. Once you reach the course, your expectations can be high. It is reasonable to expect that your game should have improved because of your investments in time and money. Then on the first tee, you hit a big slice shot out-of-bounds. Your game is as bad as ever! That first impression of how you play will most probably "flavor" the way you interpret the rest of the round. A "mind-set" of expecting to per-form badly will then be established. Since you can only play as well as you expect yourself to, this type of reaction frequently ruins your day.

Distractions, tensions, bad mind-sets, and poor expectations do not have to be part of your game–not with the proper mental attitude. I have always advised myself and other golfers to mentally "expect the worst but always hope for the best" just as physicians like myself are trained to prepare ourselves in the practice of medicine. This does not mean you should be negative in your thinking and not expect to play and score well. What it means is to be realistic about what you can do and achieve in the game.

As an example, even at the peak of my golf, I did not expect to be able to hit 300-yard drives because I have always been relatively small and thin (5 feet 8 inches tall, 130 pounds) and was quite content with drives of 230 to 250 yards. Now that I am 48 years old, still with the same body weight but with a five-year old "slipped" disc, I will be happy to be able to consistently hit drives of 200 to 220 yards. Otherwise I will constantly be unhappy during my round of golf.

Unrealistic goals that are usually beyond your capacity will only produce negative experiences and outcomes in a game that should be enjoyable and challenging. As another example, you should not be unduly disappointed if you miss a 20-foot putt by an inch or two, no matter how important it is. Even the best golfers in the world frequently miss such putts, and they play on well-manicured greens that do not make the ball bump and jump as much along the ball's path as the ones you normally play on. For putts of such distances, you should not be negative but realistic–I usually *"aim for two putts and hope for one."*

If I sink the ball on the first putt, I am delighted that I got a bonus. But if I make it in two putts, I am playing as well as I should expect, and therefore have no reason to be unhappy. On the other hand, if you aim for one putt for such distances–and usually do not succeed–you would invariably be irritated and unhappy after the first putt. This is so especially if you "overcharge" and putt the ball past the hole by more than a few feet. This negative emotional change serves as a distraction and often causes you to miss the next putt–that normally would be an easy short putt. A simple two-putt for a par now becomes an irritated three-putt bogey!

You may then continue to play poorly for the rest of the round because you continue to be upset by your frustration and apparent failure. When frustration–which often turns to anger–carries from one hole to the next it can become the mental mind-set for the remainder of the game. Negative emotions and mental perceptions are self-inflicted mental "injuries" that undo all previous teachings and good practices. They make you mentally unfit to play well.

Golf is designed to produce challenges and barriers that often are perceived to be bad breaks that happen only to you. They must be accepted as part of the game. Once a shot is played badly or you get an unlucky break, there is nothing that can be done about it. The only correct thing to do is to proceed to try to play the next and subsequent shots as well as possible. If you become excessively angry if a putt hits a spike mark or an approach shot kicks nastily off the green, your negative mental state will result in a worse score than if your reactions remained positive and constructive.

The best players in the game ignore the bad breaks and concentrate on the shot to be played. Some even welcome the bad breaks as an opportunity to execute a great recovery shot. Nothing can be done about the previous shot. One must focus on playing the next stroke as well as possible. That is why, in such circumstances, I remind myself *"Don't get mad–get even!"* Then I focus on playing well for each of the remaining shots and holes to make up for the strokes I dropped.

A major factor that will affect the mental side of your golf is the expectations or goals you have for your game. When establishing these goals, you should keep the following factors in mind:

- Goals should be challenging.
- Goals should be achievable if most and not necessarily everything you plan to do is done correctly.
- You should decide clearly what you want and have to do before you play any shot. Do not change anything once you address the ball. It is best to have a number of outcomes or goal-features for each shot (e.g., where the ball will land, how far you will follow through, the length of time you keep your head down). Even if your shot is not perfect but you achieve some of the goal-features, you will have largely been successful and should remain positive.
- You should always aim to play better but within realistic and achievable targets. This will help your concentration and focus, and keep your involvement in the game exciting. You should not play to simply maintain your standard or avoid getting worse!
- Only factors that can affect your performance should be included in the goals for a shot. It is of no advantage to merely tell ourselves to be more "determined," "focused," or "aggressive." You must actually do something (e.g, increase your concentration) or you will not be able to improve your game.
- Only use skills and techniques that you can do and are confident of reproducing well and consistently. During a round of golf, do not experiment with untried changes–they are for the practice tees and greens.

What the above points will do for you is that they will limit the game to things over which you have sufficient control. If you feel in control of what you are doing then you are more likely to be able to achieve your goals. That perception is fundamental to playing well and maintaining a good and positive mental state during a round.

THE "4Cs + 1K" PRESCRIPTION TO BETTER SCORES

This is a prescription that I developed for myself and have used successfully–and helped many of my fellow golfers–over the past 20 years of my golf experience to remind myself what I should do if I want to score or play well. The four Cs are "concentration," "confidence," "consistency," and "conservatism," and the K is the need to have a "killer" attitude or instinct.

Concentration. Although it looks easy to non-golfers, golf is such a difficult game that to play or score well, it is essential to concentrate on every shot. However, you have to learn to relax between shots to avoid becoming too tense. If that relaxation does not occur, tension would build and interfere with effective stroke making as the round progresses. The game should be one of focusing on what can be done well on every shot followed by a period of mental relaxation from the intensity of focused concentration.

Concentration is a skill that has to be learned. It is helped if you have a set routine before every shot. That routine should include making decisions (e.g., what club to use, noting environmental factors such as the lie of the landing area, the wind, and the degree of risk) and then incorporating them into a plan to make the shot (e.g., your foot placement, how to address the ball, how you will grip the club).

Mental actions like these will focus your attention on the task of striking the ball effectively. Once the routine is initiated, it should not be interrupted. The pre-shot routine should allow you to develop concentration in a manner that is familiar to you and over which you have sufficient control.

Confidence. Confidence in one's ability to perform well–the technical term is "self-efficacy"–is one of the most important principles in sports psychology that I have learned. To perform well in any sport, especially one as mental as golf, you must have confidence and truly believe (within realistic limits of course) in your ability to make a good golf shot to cross a water hazard, hit the fairway or green, or sink a putt. If you truly believe you can succeed, there is a better chance that you will. If you really believe you cannot make a particular shot or putt, or if you are hesitant about what to do, your lack of confidence will establish a self-fulfilling prophecy that usually dooms you to failure.

Confidence also involves correct club selection. Choosing the right club for the distance and circumstance of the shot will affect your prediction for success. Letting the chosen club modify the distance the ball will travel, rather than altering the more difficult feature of your skill by adjusting the swing speed or power of your shot, will simplify the nature of the game.

That is why you should take full advantage of the rule that allows you to carry 14 clubs and try to use similar types of clubs–especially where the shaft type and flex is concerned–to minimize the need to adjust your swing. You will then only be required to play with a consistent style and swing speed which means that you can become more confident in your ability to repeat good swings and shots. If every shot is altered by skill or other factors (e.g., clubs with different shaft flex), then it is unlikely you will ever develop a high degree of confidence in your swing because it always has to change.

Playing a good shot also involves using the club that you are most comfortable with, and disregarding the "advice" or comments of other golfers. It is common that as you get older and your ability changes, your choice of clubs will also change. For example, for the same distance shot, I now have more confidence in my recently-acquired 7-wood than the 4-, 5-, or even 6-iron I previously used. I disregard the frequent teasing comments from fellow golfers who are younger or stronger about having to use a wood when they only need irons. I use this as an example of my confidence in myself and my game, and that I will not let others distract me from doing what I feel most confident in. After all, it really does not matter what club you use or how you address the ball. It only matters how well you hit the ball, enjoy the game, and what score you achieve!

Since every golfer is different, part of the mental fitness of golf is learning and deciding what is right for you. It is helpful to have lessons, to read books, and to listen to others, but eventually you have to decide what is best for you to enjoy yourself, play well, and lower your score. When you are able to do that–and you should strive to do so–you will be confident in your ability to play in a manner that is suited and will produce the best results for you.

Consistency. Consistency refers to how you play a round and how you play each shot. It is not satisfying to make a par on one hole and a double-bogey on the next. That is why for putts longer than 20 feet, you should "aim for two putts and hope for one" for reasons discussed earlier in this chapter. By establishing personal "rules" like these, you can better control how you affect every shot even though they are quite different. There are two major procedures that you can follow that will affect your consistency.

The first is the development of a routine that involves mental shot preparation:

- Go through a ritualized decision-making about what club to use, where you will aim, what adjustments, if any, you need to make about that particular shot. This is the mental preparation side of the skill.
- Once the decision has been made you should then go directly into the physical portion of the shot without any interruption.
- It is common to do a transition activity to take you from the mental to the physical act. Most good golfers mentally rehearse what they will do. They do a "dry swing" of the elements of the stroke, "see" the flight of the ball, or "track" the putt until the ball rolls into the cup.
- This is a form of *"mental imagery"* you need to develop and repeat until some unconscious signal tells you to go ahead and play the actual shot. However, do not take longer than absolutely necessary and hold up play.
- The mental imagery and minor physical involvement with this type of rehearsal is a skill that has to be learned.
- It is particularly important that you clearly know what you will do before you attempt to make a stroke.

The second procedure is the development of a routine of physical actions before you actually play the shot. After your mental preparation is taken care of, the way you implement your physical actions should be standardized. Usually, this is best done as a hierarchy of experiences such as:

- Hold the club in the manner in which you have decided upon.
- When the grip feels right, proceed to the next step.
- Establish your stance so that you address the ball in the manner that you have decided upon.
- If you want to do some practice swings with the club then those swings should be as similar to the intended shot as possible. However, it is neither necessary nor desirable to make several full swings without giving your muscles sufficient time to recover.
- Any preliminary physical activities at this stage must be specific in character and directly related to the eventual shot.
- When this "practice" is satisfactory, that is, "something" tells you that everything is right to play the real stroke, move forward and address the ball.

■ *At this stage, do not change anything at this last moment.* Hit the ball in the manner that you have planned and practiced in the preparation. A last-minute change will cause you to play a shot that you have not planned for or are familiar with.

Consistency will be enhanced by a mental and physical preparation for every shot, provided you do it as quickly as possible. The more skilled and consistent you become at these preparatory phases, the more consistent will be your game. You will have reduced a major source of variability, namely, variation in shot preparation. As a bonus, the more consistent you are, the better will be your concentration and the higher will be your confidence.

Conservatism. This refers to the judgments you make about the likelihood of a particular shot being successful. An adventurous shot that is only possible if you do everything very well may yield even more trouble if it fails. For example, on a par four, if I have no more than a 60% chance of safely crossing a water hazard with the second shot and hitting the green, I would normally lay up and reduce the risks. After all there is at least a 40% chance that the shot would not clear the hazard and my score would be increased by the penalty incurred. Furthermore, it is natural that I would be irritated after failing to clear the water and this could negatively affect my next shot.

When making such decisions it is wise to consider your standard of play and then relate that to the shot difficulty. If your intentions would really stretch your ability, it is usually wiser to reassess the stroke plan. If in doubt, it is always best to be conservative in your assessments of your skill ability and play more cautiously. Once strokes are dropped, they are much more difficult to make up.

In the above example, if I had hit the ball into the water, I would incur a penalty and possibly would drop another shot after being upset by the outcome. Those two strokes dropped on that hole means that I would have to make up one stroke from two of the remaining holes. The natural tendency then would be to swing harder and "kill" the ball in an attempt to hit it further. That alteration and focus on only one part of hitting a golf ball–the power element–could be a recipe for more disaster because of a loss of control over all the important elements of the skilled movement.

It is my experience–and something that has been reinforced time and time again–that if you try to play above your true ability, the standard of your performance will usually be worse rather than better. Thus, it is good strategy not to take unnecessary risks and play safe when such risks are involved. A conservative approach to the game will at least enhance your consistency. Experienced and successful golfers know that often the secret to a lower golf score is not how many good shots you produced but how few bad ones you made in a round! Golfers who regularly bet on the outcome of their golf scores during a round of golf, also know this secret very well. That is why in such situations, the "conservatism" in golf can be replaced by other C's like "cash" or "commercial" golf

Killer attitude or instinct. This attitude or instinct is to remind you that it is important to beat the course, an opponent, or a high but real-istic standard that you have set for ourselves. If you have a too-relaxed attitude, the self-discipline that is necessary for improvement and satis-faction from playing excellence will be reduced. That will affect all the factors mentioned above–you will be less consistent–and with that comes a loss in confidence. This in turn might affect your concentration, and eventually lead you to take unnecessary risks that will yield even fur-ther disasters. A "killer" attitude is one that leads you to take the game seriously–without being unduly tense or stressed out–even though you may not be playing in an important tournament, with a person you wish to impress, your ego, or a bet.

Golf is actually such a challenging and uncompromising game that the few successes you experience become immensely enjoyable. This is one of the major factors that make "die-hard" and "crazy" golfers–of which I admit to being one–come back for more every week despite the fact that we may have had many more bad shots than good ones in our last game! The greater the number of these successes, the greater will be our satisfaction with our passion. That is why when golfers get together, non-golfers do not understand why they often keep "bragging" about the same great shot, round, or score they made. There is nothing wrong with trying to play the game as well as you possibly can on every occasion, and much to be gained from it. A killer attitude assists you to do that.

You should set targets for every round of golf in the following order of priority:

- **Enjoy yourself.** Although golf may be a passion to many, it is still a game, and should be enjoyable and satisfying rather than a matter of ego, or "life and death".
- **Try to play to your very best.** But it should always be within your own abilities taking into consideration your skill, fitness, age, experience, the weather, the course, and how you feel mentally and physically on the day of your round of golf.

- *Try to score your best.* But bear in mind that it is possible to play well but not score well (e.g., you are hitting well but had some unlucky breaks) and vice versa.
- *Play your own game.* Do not be distracted by what others are doing, or follow "friendly" advice that may cause you not to implement the "4Cs+1K" prescription described above.

SOME OTHER ACTIVITIES TO IMPROVE YOUR GOLF MENTAL FITNESS

All "die-hard" and "crazy" golfers such as I continue to play this challenging game despite its difficulties and frustrations. You are the best person to decide how much or little you enjoy your golf. It also depends very much on how you prepare ourselves mentally and physically, and whether you see golf as recreation, an assessment of your ego, a form of gambling, or a job.

As a way of increasing the enjoyment and developing a good mental approach to your game, some activities that can be pursued away from the golf course are listed below. They are explained in greater detail in Dr. Rushall's 1992 book *"Mental Skills Training For Sport"*, one of recommended references listed at the end of this book.

The following mental activities will allow you to keep golf in a healthy perspective, foster a good attitude, and contribute to your mental fitness:

- Before going to sleep at night, think in detail about three things that you do well in golf–they need not be new things.
- Upon waking in the morning, decide on at least three things you will do well that day that are associated with good golf.
- Before retiring, determine if you actually did them to the satisfactory standard that you intended.
- When thinking about your golf, concentrate on what you do well and emphasize your positive attributes.
- When thinking about your golf, you should also not see yourself as having many faults or that you frequently make errors–this is negative orientation. Rather, look on these weaknesses as areas of potential improvement–a positive orientation.
- At the same time as thinking about those improvements, determine what you need to do to achieve them.
- Whenever you think about your skills, always include what you do well and then think of what you can do to improve further.

- If you fail to concentrate on the physical or skill elements that are your strengths, in time, they could drop out of your movement pattern which will make your play worse rather than better.
- Try to develop the concept of golf as being a sequence of isolated shots–none of which interact with any other. You should then play each shot on its own merits and according to its demands.
- No shot you have played or will play should negatively affect the one that is to be played.
- Follow the priority of targets that are listed earlier in this chapter.

In conclusion, I sincerely hope that this book has provided you with sufficient tips, advice, and information to help you improve your mental and physical health and fitness so that it will assist you to enjoy and play better golf. Fitness will extend the number of years that you can play and extend your effectiveness in any round of golf. Injuries and ill-health are controllable by you to a large extent, and they should not be allowed to impinge on this most challenging, frustrating yet very enjoyable passion of ours. Happy, healthy, and better golf to you!

SOME REFERENCES AND RECOMMENDED PUBLICATIONS FOR FURTHER READING

1. American College of Sports Medicine (ACSM) Position Stand: Exercise For Patients With Coronary Artery Disease. Medicine and Science in Sports and Exercise, Vol. 23:3.1994, pages i-v.
2. July 29, 1993 Summary Statement of Workshop On Physical Activity and Public Health by the ACSM, U.S. Centers for Disease Control and Prevention, and U.S. President's Council on Physical Fitness and Sports. Sports Medicine Bulletin (Official Newsmagazine of the ACSM), Vol. 28, No. 4, 1993, page 7.
3. ACSM Position Stand: Physical Activity, Physical Fitness And Hypertension. Medicine and Science in Sports and Exercise, Vol. 25:10, 1993, pages i-x.
4. ACSM Fitness Book: Leisure Press, Champaign, Illinois, U.S.A., 1992.
5. ACSM Position Stand: The Recommended Quantity and Quality of Exercise For Developing And Maintaining Cardiorespiratory And Muscular Fitness In Healthy Adults. Medicine and Science in Sports and Exercise, Vol. 22:2, 1990, pages 265-274.
6. ACSM Position Stand: The Prevention Of Thermal Injuries During Distance Running. Medicine and Science in Sports and Exercise, Vol. 19:5. 1987, pages 529-533.
7. American Medical Association: Pocket Guide To Sports First Aid. Random House, New York, U.S.A., 1993.
8. Cooper, Kenneth H: Antioxidant Revolution. Thomas Nelson, Inc., Nashville, Tennessee, U.S.A., 1994.
9. Cooper, Kenneth H: Overcoming Hypertension. Bantam Books, New York, U.S.A., 1990.
10. Dennis, Larry: Why Your Game Should Drive You To Drink. Golf Digest, September 1991.
11. DeVincenzi P and Curtis, Suzanne: Foreplay–The Art Of Stretching. Pica La Balle, Inc. Napa, California, U.S.A., 1992.
12. Duda, Marty: Golfers Use Exercise To Get Back In The Swing. The Physician and Sports Medicine, Vol. 17, No. 8, August 1989.
13. Giam, George C K: Prevention and Treatment of Common Golf Injuries. Sports Medicine News, Vol. 2 No. 2, Sep/Oct 1993, 1-3.
14. Giam, George C K and Teh, K C: Sports Medicine, Exercise and Fitness–A Guide For Everyone. PG Publishing, Singapore, 1988.

15. Giam, George C K, Chook K K and Teh, K C: Proceedings of the 7th World Congress in Sport Psychology, 1989.

16. Golf Fit: Proper Training Will Improve Not Only Your Health But Your Handicap. Nautilus, Proline, Seattle, Washington, U.S.A.

17. Jobe, Frank W and Schwab, Diane R: 30 Exercises for Better Golf. Champion Press, Inglewood, California, U.S.A., 1986.

18. Horton, Charles E: The Most Dangerous Skin Game. Golf Digest, August 1991.

19. McCarroll J R: Golf. Chapter 14 of Sports Injuries: Mechanisms, Prevention And Treatment, Schneider R C, Kennedy J C And Plant M L, 1983.

20. McCarroll, J R and Gioe, T J: Professional Golfers And The Price They Pay. Physician and Sports Medicine, Vol. 10, No. 64, 1982.

21. McClean and Dennis: Conditioning And Warm Up. From the Golf Digest's Book of Drills, 1990.

22. McClean and Dennis: The Mental Side Of Golf. From the Golf Digest's Book of Drills, 1990.

23. Murray, Mary: Can These Pills Make You Live Longer? Reader's Digest, March 1995, pages 23-27.

24. Player, Gary: Fit For Golf–100 Exercises To Improve Your Game. Roeder Publications, Singapore, 1994.

25. Player, Gary: Golf Begins At 50–Playing The Lifetime Game Better Than Ever. Simon & Schuster, New York, U.S.A., 1989

26. Purkey, Mike: Injuries: Playing the game too hard, too long, or too wrong can lead to aches and pains in too many places. Golf Magazine, October 1993, pages 112-113.

27. Rushall, Brent S: Mental Skills Training For Sports. Sports Science Associates, 4225 Orchard Drive, Spring Valley, California 91977, U.S.A., 1992.

28. Rushall, Brent S and Pyke, Frank S: Training For Sports and Fitness. Macmillian Educational, Melbourne, Australia, 1990.

29. Saunders, H Duane: Golf & Back Pain–Does It Have To Hurt. Saunders S'ports, Minneapolis, Minnesota, U.S.A., 1992.

30. Yocum, Lewis A: Stretch Your Back. Senior Golfer, June/July 1993, pages 125-127.

INDEX

FINAL WORDS OF CAUTION AND SUGGESTIONS FROM THE AUTHOR AND PUBLISHER

CAUTION

- *"Train but don't overstrain."*
- Do not exercise until you feel actual physical pain. Remember *"exercising until you feel pain is the thinking of a person insane"*.
- Do at least five to ten minutes of warm-up aerobic and stretching exercises before you hit your first golf ball at the practice range or first tee.
- For maximum benefits and safety, exercise all parts of the body used in golf and with gradually increasing intensity. This is in accordance with the principles of gradual overload and specificity of training.

SUGGESTIONS

- It is not advisable to lend this book to other golfers because they will find it so useful for continuous reference that you won't get it back! This useful, enjoyable, and inexpensive book makes an ideal gift for your golfer friends or loved ones on either their birthday, Valentine's Day, Father's Day, Mother's Day, Christmas, graduation day or any other occasion or no occasion but just to say you care about them!
- As a suggestion, buy a copy of this book for your golfer friends (especially those who have "contributed" enough to you during your friendly bets) or tear off (or photocopy) one of the order forms provided in the next few pages for them.
- As another suggestion, you can contribute copies of this book for inclusion in the "goody bags" for golfers taking part in corporate or private tournaments you help to organize or suggest it to the organizers.
- By giving a copy of this book, you are helping your friends and fellow golfers improve their health, fitness, and golf, so that they will be able to play golf with you more frequently and for a longer time without interruptions due to ill-health, and provide you with a better challenge!

FIT-GOLF & MORE (U.S.A.)

4917 Glacier Drive, Los Angeles, California 90041-2403, U.S.A.
Tel: 1-800-9-FIT-GOLF or 1-800-934-8465
Tel: (213) 550-8886 • Fax: (213) 550-8887

Please rush me Dr. George C. Giam's 110-page book "Health & Fitness Tips To Improve Your Golf" not at the usual price of *$14.95* but at a

Special Price of $12.95 per book

(plus $3.00 per book for shipping & handling in U.S.A. & Canada.)
This offer is valid while stocks last.

Bonus: 1 free book for every 20 ordered (plus $1.50 S&H per book).

30-Day Guarantee: If not completely satisfied, please return book(s) within 30 days of delivery for full refund of Special Price.

No. of Books Ordered	Special Price	Total Price
	$12.95 per book	$
California residents: add $1.05 per book for 8.25% sales tax		$
For hard cover version : add $3.00 per book		$
For normal S&H (2-4 weeks) : add $3.00 per book		$
For faster S&H (5-7 days) : add $4.00 per book		$
20-book order S&H (2-4 weeks) : add $30.00 for 20 books		$
	TOTAL AMOUNT	$

❑ Check/money order made payable to **FIT-GOLF & MORE (U.S.A.)**

❑ Please charge to my ❑Visa ❑MC ❑Amex ❑Diners ❑Disc ❑CB

Card # ☐☐☐☐☐☐☐☐☐☐☐☐☐☐☐☐☐☐☐☐

Exp. Date:_____/_____ Signature:_____

Name:_____

Address:_____

City:_____ State:_____

Zip Code:_____ Country:_____

Tel:(____)_____ Fax:(____)_____

FIT-GOLF & MORE (U.S.A.)

4917 Glacier Drive, Los Angeles, California 90041-2403, U.S.A.
Tel: 1-800-9-FIT-GOLF or 1-800-934-8465
Tel: (213) 550-8886 ● Fax: (213) 550-8887

Please rush me Dr. George C. Giam's 110-page book "Health & Fitness Tips To Improve Your Golf" not at the usual price of *$14.95* but at a

Special Price of $12.95 per book

(plus $3.00 per book for shipping & handling in U.S.A. & Canada.)
This offer is valid while stocks last.

Bonus: 1 free book for every 20 ordered (plus $1.50 S&H per book).

30-Day Guarantee: If not completely satisfied, please return book(s) within 30 days of delivery for full refund of Special Price.

No. of Books Ordered	Special Price	Total Price
	$12.95 per book	$
California residents: add $1.05 per book for 8.25% sales tax		$
For hard cover version : add $3.00 per book		$
For normal S&H (2-4 weeks) : add $3.00 per book		$
For faster S&H (5-7 days) : add $4.00 per book		$
20-book order S&H (2-4 weeks) : add $30.00 for 20 books		$
	TOTAL AMOUNT	$

❑ Check/money order made payable to **FIT-GOLF & MORE (U.S.A.)**
❑ Please charge to my ❑Visa ❑MC ❑Amex ❑Diners ❑Disc ❑CB

Card # ☐☐☐☐☐☐☐☐☐☐☐☐☐☐☐☐☐☐☐☐

Exp. Date:_____/_____ Signature:_____

Name:_____

Address:_____

City:_____ State:_____

Zip Code:_____ Country:_____

Tel:(____)_____ Fax:(____)_____

FIT-GOLF & MORE (U.S.A.)

4917 Glacier Drive, Los Angeles, California 90041-2403, U.S.A.
Tel: 1-800-9-FIT-GOLF or 1-800-934-8465
Tel: (213) 550-8886 ● Fax: (213) 550-8887

Please rush me Dr. George C. Giam's 110-page book "Health & Fitness
Tips To Improve Your Golf" not at the usual price of **$14.95** but at a

Special Price of $12.95 per book

(plus $3.00 per book for shipping & handling in U.S.A. & Canada.)
This offer is valid while stocks last.

Bonus: 1 free book for every 20 ordered (plus $1.50 S&H per book).
30-Day Guarantee: If not completely satisfied, please return
book(s) within 30 days of delivery for full refund of Special Price.

No. of Books Ordered	Special Price	Total Price
	$12.95 per book	$
California residents: add $1.05 per book for 8.25% sales tax		$
For hard cover version : add $3.00 per book		$
For normal S&H (2-4 weeks) : add $3.00 per book		$
For faster S&H (5-7 days) : add $4.00 per book		$
20-book order S&H (2-4 weeks) : add $30.00 for 20 books		$
	TOTAL AMOUNT	$

❑ Check/money order made payable to **FIT-GOLF & MORE (U.S.A.)**
❑ Please charge to my ❑Visa ❑MC ❑Amex ❑Diners ❑Disc ❑CB

Card #

Exp. Date:_____/_____ Signature:_____

Name:_____

Address:_____

City:_____ State:_____

Zip Code:_____ Country:_____

Tel:(____)_____ Fax:(____)_____